Great Prayers of the Old Testament

Also by Walter Brueggemann from
Westminster John Knox Press

Great Prayers
of the Old Testament

Walter Brueggemann

Westminster John Knox Press
LOUISVILLE • LONDON

Scripture quotations marked NRSV are from the New Revised Standard Version of the Bible, copyright © 1989 by the Division of Christian Education of the National Council of the Churches of Christ in the U.S.A., and are used by permission. All other biblical quotations are the author's translation.

Book design by Sharon Adams
Cover design by Eric Walljasper, Minneapolis, MN

First edition
Published by Westminster John Knox Press
Louisville, Kentucky

This book is printed on acid-free paper that meets the American National Standards Institute Z39.48 standard. ∞

PRINTED IN THE UNITED STATES OF AMERICA

09 10 11 12 13 14 15 16 17 — 10 9 8 7 6 5 4 3 2

Library of Congress Cataloging-in-Publication Data

Brueggemann, Walter.
    Great prayers of the Old Testament / by Walter Brueggemann. — 1st ed.
        p. cm.
    ISBN: 978-0-664-23174-3 (alk. paper)
    1. Bible. O.T.—Prayers. 2. Prayer—Biblical teaching. 3. Bible. O.T.—Criticism, interpretation, etc. I. Title.
    BS1199.P68B78 2008
    242'.722—dc22

                                                                    2008010816

For
Sam Balentine

Contents

Acknowledgments

I am grateful to Jon L. Berquist at Westminster John Knox who initiated this volume and has seen it through to publication. I am grateful, as always, to Tia Foley, for making the enterprise of the book work. I am glad to dedicate this book to Sam Balentine, my longtime colleague and friend in scholarship. Sam has emerged as a powerful theological interpreter of Scripture with a daring theological sensibility that moves well beyond critical matters, as though this literature genuinely mattered. What I cherish most about Sam's work is that his scholarship and his life of faith are completely congruous, and one can hear it in his writings. Indeed, Sam writes the kind of stuff I would like to have written.

Walter Brueggemann
Epiphany, 2008

Introduction

Prayer in the Old Testament

Prayer is a common, ubiquitous, recurring human practice. It is the human reach toward Holy Mystery and Holy Ultimacy, an acknowledgment that human persons and human community are penultimate and stand in response to One who is scarcely accessible but who, in any case, will be addressed. In his Gifford Lectures that explore the human practice of symbol making that is made possible by "evolutionary epistemology," J. Wentzel van Huyssteen pays great attention to the Upper Paleolithic cave drawings in Southwest Europe.[1] He judges, in what I read as a compelling way, that the cave drawings are not to be categorized and dismissed simply as "primitive art." They are, rather, early attempts—as early as human persons had the psycho-physical capacity—to make contact with the world beyond human control, a world beyond that evoked and required human imagination out beyond "the given." He dares to suggest, following the work of David Lewis-Williams, that the rock wall of the cave may have been taken by those early symbol makers "as a membrane or veil between people and the spirit world," and that leads van Huyssteen to the verdict that essential elements of religion are "wired into the brain."[2]

Such a generic notion of prayer, of course, is a very long way from biblical faith, and between the generic and the biblical stands the

stricture of Karl Barth that one cannot move from "natural inclination" to the truth of the gospel. Nevertheless this insight from van
Huyssteen is an important beginning for our study. We can say that
persons in human cultures characteristically practice prayer. How
they pray, however, is determined by the particularity of the God to
whom they pray. And because Israel, in the Old Testament, prays to
the God of the exodus who is the creator of heaven and earth, we
will not be surprised that Israel prays in a certain way that is required
and permitted by the character of the God addressed.

But before we move too quickly to the particularity of Israel in
the Old Testament, we may linger over the generic a bit longer,
and that with reference to the desperate, demanding utterance of
Israel in Exodus 2:23. I focus on this utterance of ancient Israel,
because it strikes me that, as the Exodus narrative is now shaped,
this is the human utterance that begins the Exodus miracle that
stands as the core memory of Jewish imagination, core material
that has in time been taken over in Christian tradition and in
Christian practice.

In this brief narrative report, the occasion of utterance is the
death of Pharaoh, who had been abusive, ruthless, and oppressive
toward the slave community that subsequently became Israel (see
Exod. 1:8–14). During the regime of Pharaoh that slave community had seethed in silence, unable to voice the reality of its
unbearable life under the tyrannical regime of limitless productivity (Exod. 5).

But when Pharaoh died, the system of control collapsed, as it
most often does when a tyrant expires.[3] In an instant, as the news
of the death spread to the slave camps, the slave community found
its voice:

> After a long time the king of Egypt died. The Israelites
> groaned under their slavery, and cried out. Out of the slav-
> ery their cry for help rose up to God. (Exod. 2:23 NSRV)

The most remarkable matter about this cry and groan, Israel's
most elemental prayer, is that it is not addressed to anyone. One

could conclude that it is not really a prayer, since it does not intentionally address any God. But that, I take it, is the character of the most elemental prayer. Such prayer is the raw articulation of the most desperate bodily need, an out-loud utterance of unbearable suffering and misery that must be voiced. One could judge, as well, that such utterance is an act of hope, insisting that this present unbearable circumstance cannot go on any longer. One could judge that it is addressed to "an open sky," hoping that some God somewhere will hear and engage. None of that, however, is voiced in the utterance, though much may be inferred from the utterance.

In her recent narrative account "A Skeptic Learns to Pray," Lindsey Crittenden reports on her opening conversation with an Episcopal priest as she faced the violent loss of her brother.

> **LC:** But I'm a mess . . . I feel awful. . . .
>
> **Priest:** God doesn't mind. . . . Have you tried prayer?
>
> **LC:** I don't know how.
>
> **Priest:** Yes, you do. You just admitted you feel [awful]. That's a start.

Crittenden comments:

> I'd been crying out "Help" in the car and underwater in the swimming pool, where no one could hear. Desperation that blatant and raw felt embarrassing but oddly liberating and justified, too.[4]

Long before Lindsey Crittenden, Israel's prayer was just like that. The slaves, upon hearing of the death of Pharaoh, felt lousy and voiced it. It was an unthought, deeply felt cry for help. They, like Lindsey Crittenden after them, had been crying out for help while Pharaoh lived; only it had to be done so that no one would hear. Now they could risk their cry being heard! Their daring prayer is a risk and a hope, but most of all it is the voice of insistence out beyond the socially acceptable that hopes, in some inchoate way, to enlist allies in emancipation or at least in relief. Since that utterance, Israel's prayer is dominated by out-loud practice concerning unbearable circumstance in which there are no thinkable alternatives except a reach out beyond available life to whomever may be "beyond" who is capable of hearing.

The second most remarkable matter about this prayer is that it is heard. As the Israelites prayed in this raw way, they did not know if they would be heard. But they prayed anyway, because their bodies required voice.[5] The wonder of the biblical account is that "their cry rose up to God." In this verse, the God of Israel, creator of heaven and earth, is not called by name.[6] The reference to "God" here is generic, but in the context of Israel's Scripture—and Israel's engaged memory—the term "God" in serious prayer refers to the creator of heaven and earth who, in this moment of powerful exchange, becomes the God of the exodus. It is as though this God, unbeknownst to the slaves, is a magnet for the cry of wretchedness, which is a cry of hope and petition. Their cry is simply voiced; it comes to YHWH who is the target, known or unknown, of all urgent prayer. James Kugel, by his focus on Psalm 82 and its attentiveness to the weak and the needy, exposits YHWH as the one who hears such cries:

> . . . but we ought not to lose sight of our particular focus. It says that hearing the victim's cry is a god's duty and God's duty. It says that if that job is not properly performed, the very foundations of the earth will shake.[7]

> For in the Hebrew Bible, it is a frequent assertion—so frequent as to deserve the label axiomatic—that God is by nature compassionate (*ḥannun*). Indeed, this word, along with its frequent partner, "merciful" (*raḥum*), is specifically reserved for God alone: the two are never used of mere human beings in biblical Hebrew. They do, however, occur frequently in descriptions of God. He is, as noted, *axiomati-*

cally compassionate; it is simply His nature so to be. Indeed, this is what it says in what is the most important use of this pair of adjectives in the Bible, the well-known passage in chapters 33–34 of Exodus.[8]

Now, what God actually says to Moses about His being merciful is really not news—as we saw in Psalm 82, it was simply any god's job to be compassionate and merciful, and this truth was so universally assumed in the Bible that, as we have seen, it underlies the dozens of passages that speak of the victim's cry. Yet here, in Exodus, this cliché is presented as a revelation of God's ultimate self-revelation to Moses: I am by nature *ḥannun* and *raḥum* (despite all evidence to the contrary). I hear the cry of the victim; I can't help it.[9]

God hears the cry of the uncredentialed slaves! More than that, the *divine hearing* of *human prayer* mobilizes God:

God heard their groaning, and God remembered his covenant with Abraham, Isaac, and Jacob. God looked upon the Israelites, and God took notice of them. (Exod. 2:24–25)

God remembered! God looked! God saw!

Then the Lord said, "I have observed the misery of my people who are in Egypt; I have heard their cry on account of their taskmasters. Indeed, I know their sufferings, and I have come down to deliver them from the Egyptians, and to bring them up out of that land to a good and broad land, a land flowing with milk and honey, to the country of the Canaanites, the Hittites, the Amorites, the Perizzites, the Hivites, and the Jebusites. The cry of the Israelites has now come to me; I have also seen how the Egyptians oppress them." (Exod. 3:7–9)

This divine resolve, in the memory of Israel, is moved to transformative action. The *generic cry* of Israel is transposed into *a very particular hearing*, a hearing that initiates the story of God's life with Israel in the world. The belated attestation of Lindsay Crittenden is completely congruent with the early cry of the slave community. Voiced pain is not unnoticed.[10]

We have before us the *generic* and the *particular* in prayer, the generic made particular by the God to whom the prayer is received. I will consider in turn the generic and the particular. Concerning generic prayer, we may consider the classic discussion of Friedrich Heiler, who observed that prayer is, by its very character, "primitive."[11] He saw, moreover, that "primitive prayer" is an acute problem for philosophical reflection, most especially in the modern world.[12] Heiler identifies two dimensions of that problem:

1. Primitive prayer concerns "the real existence and anthropomorphic Character of the God to whom prayer is made."[13] "Primitive prayer is a real communion of man with God."[14] Prayer is intensely relational and assumes a partner who hears and responds. While God as "prayer partner" is of course unlike us, prayer assumes that there is something commensurate between the partners, namely, a capacity to communicate in dialogical fashion.

2. "Rational philosophical thought destroys the essential presuppositions of a simple prayer."[15] Heiler observes that Enlightenment rationality has made prayer impossible. In reference to Diderot (and a host of his companions), he concludes:

> The prayer of this son of the Enlightenment ends with a query which is only the cheerless expression of a restless spirit that ever questions but never affirms![16]

Thus prayer is softened in order to make intellectual accommodation and is dissolved into a good feeling:

> Another reinterpretation is frequently given to prayer by making it a mere recollection of God or the symbol of a pious disposition, a humble and grateful mood, a trusting and lov-

ing heart. The element in prayer which is objectionable to
the philosopher, the thought of an influence brought to bear
on God is accordingly set aside, the objective, metaphysical
character of prayer is obliterated, and the significance which
is admitted is purely subjective and psychological.[17]

In the end, however, Heiler concludes that such philosophical
reductionism, even in its more popular forms of prayer as a psychological transaction (the self with the self) or "New Age"
generic religiosity, cannot dispel the impulse to pray:

> The philosophical ideal of prayer has become practical only
> within the narrow limits of a philosophical school; it has
> never touched the outer circles of ordinary men and women.
> It possesses no constructive energy; it can produce only dis-
> solving and destroying effects. But as little as rites and incan-
> tations could stifle simple prayer, so little can philosophical
> criticism kill it. Life in its irrational defiance shows itself
> stronger than thought in its uncompromising logicality.
> There arises an inner necessity for man to pray: "to be a
> human being—that means to pray." The distresses of life are
> too heavy, the will to live too strong, the liberating and con-
> soling power of prayer too wonderful for man to be able to
> satisfy himself with the chill prayer of a philosophical ideal.
> Natural prayer is indestructible. By its power and passion it
> lives in all lands and times; still more wonderfully and more
> powerfully it lives in the devotional life of great religious
> personalities. The delineation of their life of prayer only
> reveals the philosophical ideal of prayer in all its coldness, its
> lack of life and substance.[18]

What Heiler has understood critically and reflectively is completely evident in Israel's practice, and in the textual attestations of
Israel's practice. It is clear that Israel's speech toward God expressed
in the regularities of the Psalter is the *speech of extremity* that pushes
beyond rational, explanatory discourse out into its ecstasy and its

agony. On the one hand, Israel's praise consists in exuberant, glad, trusting self-abandonment as the community cedes itself over in wonder, love, and praise to the goodness and transformative rule of YHWH.[19] In common discourse, "praise" is usually recognized in Old Testament study as the opposite of "prayer," which takes the form of lament, protest, complaint, and petition. But the full discourse of Israel with YHWH perforce includes doxology and the magnification of YHWH through Israel's songs.[20]

But on the other hand, Israel's *speech of extremity* is the petitionary prayer of lament and protest that also pushes readily beyond explanatory modes into needful, desperate, hopeful address. It is clear that Israel's petitionary utterances assume that this is a genuine dialogical transaction that is not a psychological exercise, but a real exchange between engaged agents:

> Can we therefore conclude that the Hebrew term "mediation" suggests something like romantic self-consciousness— a self-consciousness that expresses itself essentially in monologue? The answer is that the Psalms are not monologues but insistently and at all times dialogue-poems, poems of the self but of the self in the mutuality of relationship with the other. . . . To speak of relationality pure and simple is, however, misleading. The Psalms are not exercises in existential philosophy; we are not speaking of other and of the self in relation to the other. The "Thou" *answers* the plea of the "I" and that answer signals a change in the opening situation. The Psalms are in this sense dynamic, they involve action, purpose. W. H. Auden said in his elegy on the death of Yeats, "For poetry makes nothing happen." This is not true of the Psalms. In nearly every psalm something does happen. The encounter between the "I" and the "Thou" is the signal for a change not merely in the inner realm of consciousness but in the realm of outer events.[21]

It is evident in contemporary church practice, given rational assumptions and psychological sophistication, that much prayer in the church is reduced to an emotional exercise. This is evident in our propensity to "feel better" when we pray, and in the readiness to water down petitions so as not to ask in bold ways, when our modernity assumes that in fact there is no one listening anyway.

Such embarrassment about the "primitive" quality of prayer is regularly overcome, however, when otherwise "rational and modern" people who eschew the "primitive" are propelled into "regressive" speech by the reality of circumstance that is unbearable and that must be brought to voice. Every pastor knows how it is, in such an emergency, that the silence is broken and the speech of faith "descends" into a cry and a demand, because such speech lies at the heart of faith. When faithful people "descend" into such regressive, urgent, demanding, sometimes shrill and rude speech, contemporaries are simply reentering the world of ancient Israel which is a world of prayer that is not yet disciplined or restrained by the rational limits of modernity.

In that ancient world to which Jews and Christians are heirs, prayer is a defining and indispensable activity. As a result, Israel has collected its prayers (along with its praise) in the book of Psalms. Behind that, however, in a way that is the subject of the following discussion, Israel's prayers regularly occur in the midst of narrative. It is as though transactions with YHWH are so defining for Israel that Israel cannot tell its story without reference to prayer. Prayer is a vehicle whereby the power and compassion of YHWH are emergent in the narrative. Without that emergent, moreover, this would not be Israel's story, because Israel's story has the presence and power of YHWH at its center. Thus it is evident that Israel's prayer, over time, is highly stylized. That is why a study of genre (since the time of Hermann Gunkel) is the beginning point of critical study of prayer in Israel.[22] Israel reiterated patterns of speech, and in the reiteration regularly ordered its experience and "contained" the extremities of its experience in approved, socialized forms of utterance.[23] Thus its prayers are a dramatic practice and a social constriction and reconstruction, so that the practitioners of familiar prayer patterns could be confident that their own voiced experience belonged appropriately with the horizon of Israel's faith. Every dimension of Israel's life is lived before YHWH in practiced, welcome, and legitimated regularized liturgical usage.[24]

Given that stylization, however, what strikes one about the prayers of Israel (even more than its acts of praise) is the remarkable particularity of the utterances. While praise could be quite stereotypical in the Old Testament, prayers of lament and complaint are notably imaginative in the extremity of language and in the risk of venturesome image and metaphor. While such prayers are disciplined by and situated in common recurring patterns, there is never doubt that the prayer is that of a particular person in a particular time and place, someone who is able to take what is stylized and appropriate in compelling ways. This permeation of *the stylized* by *the particular* serves both ancient and contemporary community. A study of the text in the ancient world permits us to see that the particularity of prayer reflects a person in a namable context. Thus the prayer is particularly that of Jacob or of Moses or Jeremiah. It is that same particularity that permits contemporary users of the prayers to appropriate them as one's own prayer. Thus the contemporary voice of prayer may pray after Jacob or after Moses or after Jeremiah. But clearly the prayer is *my prayer* and *our prayer* in this time and place. And because the prayer is situated in a context of crisis, there is nothing trivial or routine about it, as the voice of prayer must find an articulation that is congruent with present need and with present hope.

In both ancient practice and contemporary practice, prayer is a daring act. It is an act that intends to connect present *urgent context* with *sovereign compassionate holiness*. This is not an easy exercise, but one that requires great faith and courage, even *chutzpah*. The contact made between context and holiness, wherein one's life is at stake, is the quintessence of prayer, but that does not make contact easy. The delicacy of such contact is exhibited in Michelangelo's Sistine Chapel rendering of Adam "touching" God, or in the church's practice of the Eucharist, in which the bread of the earth becomes the bread of heaven and the fruit of the vine becomes the blood of Christ. The church's long-time dispute about "real presence" indicates how problematic the contact is. What we see as tension in Michelangelo and as dispute in the church on Eucharist is in play each time we pray, the daring transaction in which our life is at stake. It would be safer (better?) not to pray. Except that we (and the characters whose prayers we study in what follows) are not unlike Lindsay Crittenden who feels lousy, not unlike Pharaoh's slaves who cry out . . . because their bodies can no longer be silent in submission. We may hone and smooth and edit (censor!) prayer into proper liturgical form, but the urgency will nonetheless break the silence and, along with the silence, break the imposed nicety of manner that requires the silence. Israel's prayer is a refusal to accept that silence that is most often oppressive and that works to preclude human freedom and human well-being.[25]

There is a great deal of literature on prayer in the Old Testament. I will refer to four studies that have been instructive for my own work.[26] First, Moshe Greenberg in 1983 published a most important study of prayer that is offered in biblical prose, an enterprise not unlike what follows in this book.[27] Greenberg's study is of immense interest; among other things he tracks the typical stylization of prayers in the Hebrew Bible, and refutes the judgments of modernity that have been imposed on the prayers in much recent interpretation. He takes seriously the fact that such prayers are *real transactions* between engaged partners:

> Speaking in the second person is only the most elemental form of biblical man's speech to God. When he prays, he uses words in patterns, and these patterns follow the analogy of interhuman speech patterns in comparable situations. The interhuman situation of petition may be analyzed as comprising the following elements: a need or distress; an unequal division of goods between petitioner and petitioned, leading the former to resort to the latter; affirmation of the given relationship between the two: the petitioner does not intend to destroy the relationship (he does not come with a club to take the goods by force), but to maintain himself on its basis;

reliance on some common interest, some ground for solidarity between the two (else why should the petitioned be
moved at all to part with his goods, or even to share them,
for the benefit of the petitioner?[28]

The fact that the one who prays seeks "common interest" with the
God addressed indicates that such prayer is not a practice of abdi-
cating deference, but is a genuine engagement that proposes a
new worldly possibility:

The pray-er needs a good that only God can bestow. He
appeals to God on the basis of an established relation with
him, which he invokes in several ways: by aptly chosen epi-
thets and descriptive attributes, and especially in the moti-
vating sentence. In the motivation, the pray-er appeals to a
common value, some identity of interest between him and
God, some ground on which he can expect God's sympathy
and a demonstration of solidarity. Thus all the elements sur-
rounding the petition, before it and after it, aim at establish-
ing a bond between the pray-er and God, an identity of
interest—a primary aim of prayer rhetoric.[29]

It is fair to say, I believe, that Greenberg brings such clarity to the
transactive quality of prayer precisely because he reads as a Jew.
Much Christian piety and prayer are far too polite and deferential. Christians, in my judgment, must continue to learn from Jews
about the gravity required in prayer that bespeaks the legitimacy
of the petitioner.

Ronald Clements has provided a study of prayer in the Old Testament that offers, almost exclusively, careful exegesis of specific
texts.[30] His exposition of texts is reliable and illuminating. In his
introduction, Clements identifies three ways in which prayer shows
the "spiritual significance" of events being related in the text:

In the first place such prayers often open up a disclosure of
the inner hopes of the individual whose work is being

described. We come to see that there is an outer history, which the archivist and archaeologist can bring to our attention through research. Beside this stands an inner history which belongs to the realm of faith and spiritual understanding. This the prayer can reveal. Secondly we find that in some cases the inclusion of a prayer may indicate how the events being described fit into the divine scheme. The prayer becomes a kind of spiritual connective, indicating the path that God's providential purpose is following. Thirdly we can claim that it is the element of prayer, and with it the whole sense of a communion between humans and God to which it bears witness, that makes the biblical story a truly religious and spiritual one.[31]

Clements, moreover, acknowledges that prayer is an act of imagination that in its construal of lived reality goes beyond the obvious in its perception through the eyes of faith:

Just as a skillful playwright can use the speeches which various actors make in order to uncover the plot of a drama, so does the Bible use the prayers of its central figures to show that the eyes of faith can discover a purpose in human life and history. In turn such discovery makes possible new directions and new achievements in our world and society.[32]

It is clear in such prayer that in detailing for God the circumstance of need, the speaker not only describes, but lets the prayer serve as a trope of imagination. Such a recurring practice suggests that Israel understood that as an Israelite can exercise imaginative freedom in such communication, so the God addressed is also an agent of imagination who can reperceive and redescribe reality in transformative ways.

The third study is the detailed and erudite offer of Patrick D. Miller, who has shaped his discussion according to genre analysis, but has unpacked Israel's use of familiar genres in wonderfully suggestive ways.[33] After the introductory work of Greenberg and

Clements, Miller does "the heavy lifting" of close exposition. By attention to the detail of rhetoric, Miller exhibits the powerful and consistent theological passion of Israel at prayer. In his final chapter Miller considers the way in which Old Testament prayers become a primary legacy to the New Testament and to the church.[34] He considers prayer in Trinitarian, christological, and ecclesiological usage. As a plus, he offers a splendid exposition of the Lord's Prayer.

The fourth study is that of Samuel Balentine, who takes full advantage of newer methods of interpretation that permit him to focus on the dramatic, interactive practice of prayer.[35] By close textual reading, he is able to sketch out the "characters" that participate in prayer, and most especially the character of God in the work of compassion and justice. It is inevitable that in such a consideration, Balentine must come face-to-face with the issue of theodicy. Israel knows, as Balentine makes clear, that after all the trusting petitions to YHWH and after assurances about YHWH's attentive compassion, the stark reality of faith is that prayer is not always answered and evil persists, even among the faithful. In the end, Balentine's discussion makes unmistakably clear that prayer is an act of dialogue in which both parties have an active role to play:

> When the church encourages the practice of lament, it promotes an understanding of divine-human communion or partnership where radical dialogue is both normative and productive. True covenant relationship like that which is struck at Sinai involves the mutual participation of two partners. The partnership is clearly between persons of unequal power and authority. God is *the* creator, and God is *the* covenant maker. But in the Hebraic notion of covenant, God is not the only one with power, not the only one having a voice in what is to take place. The human partner also has a say. On occasion the human voice speaks with words of praise and thanksgiving, signaling not only consent to the divine will but also grateful submission. But on those occa-

sions when the hurt and pain of life do not permit a simple "Yes" or a manufactured "Hallelujah," Israel does not retreat into passive silence. On these occasions the dialogue calls for lament and the covenant relationship permits it—indeed, even requires it.

The point here is that covenant relationship, like human relationships, requires communication. The better the communication, the better the relationship, that is, the healthier it is and the more possibilities it has for growth and development. In the same way, restricted communication or, worse, silence reduces the possibilities within the relationship.[36]

Finally in this summary of important literature on prayer in the Old Testament, I conclude with reference to Karl Barth. In addition to his more extended discussion in *Church Dogmatics*, he has written a small book in which he summarizes his larger argument.[37] I accent two points from Barth that are quintessential for the prayers considered in this volume. First, Barth asserts that prayer is "asking":

In the first instance, it is an asking, a seeking and a knocking directed towards God; a wishing, a desiring and a requesting presented to God. And the actuality of prayer is decidedly against not merely a precedence of the other two elements but even their equality with petition. The man who really prays comes to God and approaches and speaks to Him because he seeks something of God, because he desires and expects something, because he hopes to receive something which he needs, something which he does not hope to receive from anyone else, but does definitely hope to receive from God. He cannot come before God with his petition without also worshipping God, without giving Him praise and thanksgiving, and without spreading out before Him his own wretchedness. But it is the fact that he comes before God with his petition which makes him a praying man. Other theories of prayer may be richly and profoundly thought out and may sound very well, but they all suffer from a certain artificiality because they miss this simple and concrete fact, losing themselves in heights and depths where there is no place for the man who really prays, who is simply making a request.[38]

At the center of prayer is petition. It will be clear in the prayers considered herein that petition is the center toward which all parts of the rhetoric move. In like manner Clements asserts:

> Certainly we can begin to look at the central forms of prayer which the Bible contains by concerning ourselves with petition. "Ask, and it will be given you" (Luke 11:9), seems at first glance to sum up all that we mean by prayer. It is wholly in line with this then to find that simply to "ask" God for something becomes a basic expression for prayer.[39]

Clements's reference to Luke 11:9 evidences that Jesus is exactly committed to "asking," for asking makes explicit the proper and defining relation of Israel (and the world) to God. Israel's practice is one of need and hope; God's response is one of attentive abundance. All prayer proceeds on this basis, even when there is protest that God's abundance is lacking and not visible.

Second, Barth can say:

> God is not deaf, but listens; more than that, he acts. God does not act in the same way whether we pray or not. Prayer exerts an influence upon God's action, even upon his existence. . . . But one thing is beyond doubt: it is the answer that God gives. Our prayers are weak and poor. Nevertheless, what matters is not that our prayers be forceful, but that God listens to them. That is why we pray.[40]

This judgment by Barth is remarkable for this master theologian who has spent his life witnessing to the "otherness" of God. Here Barth discloses his evangelical passion by attesting that human life can impinge upon this "other God" and recruit God into the life of the world. This affirmation by Barth, at the end of my discussion, is fully congruent with the "cry" of Exodus 2:23 that we have seen as the beginning of prayer in Israel. Israel, before God, is needful and hopeful. The evangelical claim of the text is that God is attentive, available, responsive, and generous in response. Israel could remember past divine fidelities, and so could petition and intercede for present and future fidelities as well, for without that divine fidelity the life of Israel and the life of the world end without hope and without possibility.[41] Israel, in its passion, and without great critical reflection, knows this. It knows this in its instructional tradition. But beyond that, it knows it in its bodily reality, rendering itself needfully back to the creator who continues to recreate.

In what follows I have not gone very far in articulating the urgent contemporaneity of these prayers, though I assume much of that is implicit in my comment and will be evident to the reader. I stress, in the end, that the most characteristic prayers of ancient Israel operate in a juridical frame of reference; in that frame of reference God is known to be committed to justice and well-being; Israel at prayer pleads for the justice and well-being of YHWH that have not yet been enacted. The point of contemporaneity in the juridical plot of prayer is that the prayers of the faithful are now offered in a world that is terribly skewed, permeated with violence, brutality, and injustice. While the questions of theodicy are acute for the faithful, the faithful, then and now, continue to pray for a transformed world, even if much of our petition and intercession are quite personal and intimate. Such prayers for a transformed world are crucial on at least three counts:

1. Such prayer serves in vigorous ways to counter the *idolatry* all around us that assumes human ultimacy that ends either in pride or in despair. In a world of human self-congratulations, prayer enacts a zone of freedom for covenantal interaction in which one need not be in control. The dominant focus in our society wants to nullify any zone of freedom and create an environment of necessity—necessary productivity, necessary fear and

anxiety, necessary aggressiveness. Prayer is a refusal to give our lives over to such idolatrous necessity.

2. Prayer as an act and posture of dependence on God serves to counter a pervasive sense of *self-sufficiency* that is available in and fostered by the nurture of "development" that takes place through ideology, propaganda, and advertising. Our Western developed world is bent on Promethean exuberance that does immense violence to the neighborhood and that cannot be sustained. Prayer is an act of engagement with an immense Other, a combination of praise and deference, but also an insistence that refuses the characteristic pride of Western arrogance. Israel can be honest and insistent in its need, but can still acknowledge before the God it addresses, that its proper place is before the mystery of God:

> O Lord, my heart is not lifted up,
>   my eyes are not raised too high;
> I do not occupy myself with things
>   too great and too marvelous for me.
>   (Ps. 131:1 NRSV)

3. Israel at prayer is committed to a *dialogic existence* with God in which both parties are free and both parties are at risk. Such prayer serves to counter the enormous temptation to monologue that causes a nullification of the human spirit. Monologue is everywhere among us—in absolute theology, absolute patriotism, absolute authority, absolute autonomy—any practice that assures that we can live without being decisively impinged upon by "the other." In Israel's purview, the neighbor is one who impinges as "other." And behind the neighbor stands God, who impinges on life and who will be impinged upon by Israel at prayer. Such a dialogic mode of existence admits of no final settlement, but only an ongoing interaction that invites always to new speech and to new freedom, trust, and responsibility. Israel is relentlessly dialogic, in its discernment and practice of reality, and so stands as a mighty alternative to all monologues.[42] In the end, prayer as utterance is

a refusal of silence, for every settled authority wants to silence dissenting inconvenience. The out-loud tradition of Israel is important in the contemporary world, and the rediscovery of speech among the silenced is urgent.

I finish with two occasions in the memory of Jesus concerning silence and speech. In both episodes, the issue of urgent petition is in response to a skewed world, the first a physical disability, the second an economic disability. First, in Mark 10:46–52, the blind beggar Bartimaeus seeks healing from Jesus. He cried out in what was not unlike a petitionary prayer:

> When he heard that it was Jesus of Nazareth, he began to shout out and say, "Jesus, Son of David, have mercy on me!" (Mark 10:47 NRSV)

It does not surprise us that he was silenced:

> Many sternly ordered him to be quiet . . . (Mark 10:48 NRSV)

Nor does it surprise us that in his need he refused to be silenced; he knew that in his silence he would never receive help:

> but he cried out even more loudly, "Son of David, have mercy on me!" (Mark 10:48 NRSV)

The narrative reports that his cry and his refusal of silence evoked the healing of Jesus. But it required a resolute vigorous petition for mercy!

Second, in Luke 18:1–8 Jesus tells a parable about the "need to pray always and not to lose heart" (v. 1 NRSV). The parable concerns a widow who asked for justice. As expected, the judge refused, as judicial actions move slowly and without responsiveness. But she "kept coming." She kept petitioning the court. She kept at it so long that the judge finally granted her petition:

yet because this widow keeps bothering me, I will grant her
justice, so that she may not wear me out by continually coming. (Luke 18:5 NRSV)

The widow did not lose heart! Jesus intended that his disciples
would not lose heart, and so should pray always; the military-
consumer culture, by contrast, wants us to lose heart; because
when we lose heart, we pursue commodities and safety and control. This community of faith, both Jewish and Christian, prays
out loud in bold ways. It does not lose heart. Instead, it receives
transformed life from the God who . . . sometimes . . . hears and
answers.

Chapter One

Abraham

Genesis 18:22–33

Abraham, father of faith, appears abruptly in the narrative. He has a traceable pedigree going back to Shem, son of Noah (Gen. 11:10–32). But his emergence in the book of Genesis is nonetheless abrupt because he is the first in his family and the first in Israel to be directly addressed by God (Gen. 12:1–3). He is addressed, without explanation, by the summons of God, who speaks to him a life-shattering imperative: "Go!" The divine summons is to put Abraham into pilgrimage, at risk, toward a land he does not know. Beyond that, he is to be a bearer of divine blessing, a historical figure through whom the life-giving energy and goodness of God are mediated and made available in the world. Wherever Abraham will go, the chance for life from God is palpably on offer.

Remarkably, without discussion or explanation or expression of any curiosity, Abraham obeys the divine summons and departs (Gen. 12:4). His departure is as abrupt as was the intrusive divine address. The account of the departure from Haran features Abraham as the head of a great tribal movement, the one responsible for the safety and well-being of all members of the tribe. Two details may be noted in his departure. First, he departs with all "his possessions" and "persons," perhaps slaves. He is a man of substance with some important social significance and gravitas.

1

Second, among his company is his nephew Lot, son of Haran. It is evident that Lot will figure in the story to come, for he is mentioned twice (vv. 4–5).

In common tradition (and certainly in New Testament attestation), Abraham is reckoned as an exemplar of faith (see Rom. 4:16–25; Gal. 3:6–9). He is portrayed as one who trusted God's promise (Gen. 15:6), most especially in his readiness to obey the divine command in the sacrificial offering of his only son (Gen. 22:12). That commendation of Abraham, however, is more than a little qualified if we read the fine print of the narrative. In Genesis 12:10–20 he is prepared to sacrifice his wife Sarah to Pharaoh's desire in order to keep his life safe (see Gen. 20:1–18). And in his troubled dealing with his triangle with Sarah and Hagar, he is presented in a less than favorable light (Gen. 16:1–6). Alongside his celebrated faith, Abraham is also portrayed as a practical man who is capable of looking out for his own interests.

His particular interaction with his nephew Lot exhibits Abraham's concern for and his generosity toward his kinsman; it also reflects his enormous wealth as head of the clan. When the flocks and herds of the two became plentiful, there was a dispute over water and grazing rights. And Abraham adjudicates the matter peaceably by permitting his nephew to pick the best part of the land:

> Then Abram said to Lot, "Let there be no strife between you and me, and between your herders and my herders; for we are kindred. Is not the whole land before you? Separate yourself from me. If you take the left hand, then I will go to the right; or if you take the right hand, then I will go to the left. (Gen. 13:8–9 NRSV)

Lot, it is reported, chose and settled in "the cities of the Plain and moved his tent as far as Sodom" (Gen. 13:12 NRSV).

By the time we reach our text in Genesis 18, our proper focus of study, the narrative of Abraham has a much bigger scope. Now Abraham has in his purview the city of Sodom to which Lot had moved. The context for the great prayer of Abraham is a juxtaposition of two incompatible features. On the one hand, *Sodom*—where Lot resides—is filled with "wicked, great sin" that has evoked "an outcry." The cause of the cry is not narrated, but characteristically an "outcry" is evoked by a miscarriage of justice, perhaps an act of oppression or exploitation, sometimes-personal brutality, often-economic exploitation. This status of Sodom is matched against Abraham's status as the *intimate of YHWH*. The narrative suggests that Abraham and YHWH share confidences and are perhaps "best friends," or as Isaiah 41:8 has it, "Abraham, my friend." More than that, Abraham is here, as nowhere else in Genesis, identified as the one who will do "righteousness and justice." Thus *righteousness and justice on the part of Abraham, an outcry against the great sin of Sodom* on the other. The narrative constructs a perfect tension! Something must give! And it "gives" as Abraham addresses YHWH in demanding, insistent prayer.

The prayer of Abraham in verses 22–32 is framed with a narrative introduction (v. 22) and a narrative conclusion (v. 33). The introduction is of peculiar interest because it may offer us one of the most important comments in all of Scripture concerning prayer. The conventional text, as in the NRSV, describes Abraham as "standing before YHWH." The picture is of Abraham as a suppliant, in a posture of a petitioner, perhaps not unlike a suppliant who is ushered in to see the Godfather with a particular request. Such a scene would suggest that Abraham is deferential toward the God whom he approaches, and asks for that to which he is not entitled, asking at some risk. The God whom he approaches is awesome and perhaps not too much inclined to grant favors to those who have no bargaining power. All of this is quite conventional, for prayer before the God of the Bible is offered by those with empty hands (see Luke 18:13).

Such a construal of this meeting, however, is called into question by the fact that verse 22 contains a "scribal correction" (noted in the NRSV as "another ancient tradition"). In fact that alternative tradition suggests that an earlier form of the narrative had "YHWH standing before Abraham," to suggest that Abraham was the senior partner and YHWH a deferential suppliant, with roles reversed. Thus the "earlier text" proposes that the positions of the two parties are reversed; Abraham holds the upper hand in the transaction, as though YHWH were approaching Abraham, "hat in hand." This textual change may be the most important matter in this narrative, for it invites us to rethink the "posture of prayer" and the way we may be situated before God, as deferential suppliant (as is usual) or as senior party to the transaction with immense gravitas. This positioning of Abraham perhaps better prepares us for the prayer of Abraham that is to follow.

The "scribal correction" is one of eighteen where the ancient scribes have altered the text—and have indicated that they have done so—because they have found the theological implication of the text to be unacceptable. The change is not a copying error, but a deliberate theological-interpretive "correction." In this case it was judged to be unacceptable that God would "stand before" Abraham as the lesser party to the transaction. The scribes have altered the text to bring the narrative into conformity with conventional theological opinion. But against the judgment of the scribes, we may at least pause to entertain the dramatic alternative, that in some contexts of prayer the petitioner is bold enough and daring enough to proceed as though the petitioner held the initiative to which God must respond. In a dramatic encounter such as the one offered here, there is no excessive deference before God; rather, there is an urgency that is grounded in indignation, which marks the tone of the prayer that follows. Abraham, YHWH's best friend, stands before God with some sense of entitlement, a daring posture for prayer, but one grounded in the interactive, covenantal relationship that Abraham has with YHWH.

The prayer itself may be divided into two sections, an initial *confrontation* (vv. 23–25) and the *negotiations* that follow (vv. 26–32). In the initial confrontation, only Abraham speaks. His utterance consists in two questions, followed by two statements, concluded with one more question, the sum of which amounts to a reprimand and a reminder to YHWH of YHWH's proper conduct.

The first question anticipates what YHWH intends to do when

YHWH checks out the sin of Sodom (v. 23). The assumption is that YHWH will destroy the city wholesale. Abraham does not doubt YHWH's capacity to "sweep away" the entire city. YHWH's power is never in question. But Abraham qualifies YHWH's free use of power by the introduction of the ethical-covenantal-legal categories of "righteous-wicked." YHWH, so Abraham assumes, intends to make no ethical distinction; Abraham insists—against YHWH's indiscriminate resolve—that ethical distinctions must be made. God is obligated to differentiate between the wicked (guilty) who disregard God and violate neighbor and the righteous (innocent) who fear God and honor neighbor. God is pressed by Abraham to curb divine power enough to draw distinctions. It is as though Abraham instructs YHWH.

The second question, on the assumption of fifty righteous (innocent) persons in the city, is whether divine destruction will make no allowances (v. 24). The second question reiterates the concern of the first, but now advances beyond it with an introduction of "forgiveness" (*ns'*). In this probe, Abraham suggests not only that the assumed fifty righteous be rescued, but that they be the basis for rescue of the entire city. This remarkable assertion shows biblical faith and biblical prayer on their way to the conviction that a life well lived may be a mode of rescue of the others, an insight that in Christian tradition will eventuate in an affirmation about the saving significance of the life of Jesus, the singularly righteous man. That is, the innocent may outweigh the earned punishment of the guilty. In his prayer Abraham urges YHWH to take a leap of generosity toward the wicked city. As in the first question, there is no divine response.

The first assertion, following the two questions, begins with an exclamatory word derived from the term for pollute, or defile. Our usual rendering in the verse, "Far be it from you," is a weak translation that does not hint at the seriousness of the term. It might better be rendered in context, "It would be defiling of you," or "It would make you polluted." The warning Abraham issues to YHWH is that to enact wholesale judgment on the city without regard to the innocent would violate YHWH's own holiness, for "holiness" (*qdš*) is the antithesis of the term "profane" (*hll*). That is, such an action would contradict YHWH's deepest core trait; it would cheapen, trivialize, and violate who YHWH is known to be in Israel. YHWH, in YHWH's holiness, is responsible for making discriminating judgments, and is about to forfeit that character and that reputation.

The second assertion in verse 25, again with the term *hll* (pollute, defile), simply reiterates the point. The additional rhetoric is designed to seal the case.

The concluding question at the end of verse 25 is Abraham's trump card as he summons YHWH to better performance. In order to sense the rhetorical force of the question it is necessary to recognize that in Hebrew the words "judge" and "justice" derive from the same root, *shapat* and *mišpat*. YHWH is acknowledged to be the judge of all the earth. Abraham does not question YHWH's capacity for governance or authority to rule. YHWH is about to render an indiscriminate verdict, as though YHWH were a "hanging judge" who is not interested in evidence brought before the court. But such a verdict and sentence would be a gross miscarriage of justice. Thus attention must be paid to the innocent. They matter to the conduct of the court. Abraham is thus the great intercessor who functions as "a friend of the court" who can ask the judge to refrain from judgment that goes too far. It is obvious that in the prayer thus far, Abraham is the initiator and senior partner. We have not yet heard from YHWH.

In the negotiations that follow, YHWH speaks and agrees to pursue Abraham's line of argument (vv. 26–32). At the outset of the negotiation, YHWH grants Abraham's premise: the presence of fifty innocents in the city will be enough to save the city. Now YHWH uses the same word for "forgive" (*ns'*) earlier utilized by Abraham. Thus far the prayer of Abraham is effective. YHWH has agreed to Abraham's point of view.

But then it is as if Abraham begins to lack confidence in the premise of his argument. He is now less than sure that there are fifty innocents in Sodom. He begins to bargain. What follows is like an auction to see what the best available price may be. The tone of the interaction is like the bargaining in a Near Eastern bazaar in which contesting the price is part of the "game." Thus we may judge that there is something playful in the prayer. Once YHWH has conceded Abraham's argument, the two parties seem at ease with a classic Jewish transaction of seeking the best deal.

Abraham's second bid is to lower the requirement of the number of innocents from fifty to forty-five because Abraham now has a hunch that he could not find fifty innocents in the city. This offer is made with a play of humility, "dust and ashes," an ingratiating phrase that recruits the assent of the "seller." YHWH, in his response, is a vigorous but responsive bargainer, and will go down to forty-five. The bargaining continues. The two parties can agree to forty as the required quota. In such bazaar bargaining, however, one is never sure one has reached the limit. No one knows ahead of time how far the matter can be pressed. Abraham will try one more time for a smaller number, but he must now tread into risky territory. He might offend the judge and so qualifies his request with the hope that the judge will not be affronted. But the judge is agreeable, and accepts the new offer. Now in verse 31 it is as though Abraham asks permission to go one step further, down to twenty; again the judge agrees. And in verse 32, Abraham acknowledges that he will speak "one last time" . . . final offer! In this series of exchanges, the most interesting rhetoric is Abraham's growing deference toward YHWH:

- dust and ashes (v. 27)
- do not be angry (v. 30)
- let me speak again (v. 31)
- do not be angry (v. 32)

The rhetoric gives the impression that Abraham has daringly pushed the envelope as far as he can. By contrast to the speech of Abraham, YHWH is laconic in speech and offers only terse, albeit affirmative, responses. YHWH engages Abraham, and assents to his request and his bargaining offers. Apparently Abraham will not, dares not, go lower than ten. We are not told why, though one thought is that ten constitutes a Jewish minion, the required number of Jewish men for a legitimate transaction with God. In context, perhaps, Abraham decided that to push farther is unreasonable, so disproportionate is such a number to the throngs of the wicked in Sodom.

In any case, the meeting ends, the prayer is terminated. The two parties have reached an understanding. Abraham has moved YHWH toward readiness to forgive, evidencing that the justice of the judge will indeed be marked by mercy. But Abraham had to concede that the innocent have only limited saving power; they cannot override the dense reality of wickedness. It is clear that while the prayer ends, this is not the last exchange Israel must have with God concerning justice, wrath, mercy, and forgiveness. The exchange exhibits Abraham as a daring man of faith. More importantly, it presents YHWH as a ready and available partner in the free play of prayer in which the destiny of the world hangs in the balance and is under intense negotiation.

The prayer is ended, but life goes on after the prayer has been concluded. In the narrative that follows in Genesis 19:1–29, it is clear that the divine intent to destroy Sodom has not been deterred by the prayer of Abraham. No comment is made about any righteous persons in the city. The city will be "consumed" because the "outcry" is great (19:15). The inspection of the city by YHWH that was anticipated in 18:21 has established that the city has failed in its wickedness; the holy God—undefiled—will not tolerate the defilement. The destruction by "sulphur and fire" and the "overthrow" of the city are unqualified (vv. 24–25). Thus the narrative establishes that the judge has acted justly, for neither the narrator nor Abraham offers any comment to the contrary.

There is, almost incidentally, mitigation in the wholesale slaughter that may be credited to Abraham. Lot and his family are warned and advised to leave in order to avoid the coming disaster (19:15–23). The narrative ends with reference to Abraham:

So it was that, when God destroyed the cities of the Plain, God remembered Abraham, and sent Lot out of the midst of the overthrow, when he overthrew the cities in which Lot had settled (Gen. 19:29 NRSV).

YHWH remembered Abraham, remembered Abraham's fidelity and YHWH's commitment to him. YHWH remembered Abraham in the same way that YHWH remembered Noah (Gen. 8:1) and remembered Rachel (Gen. 30:22) to their good. It is not said anywhere that Lot is righteous or that he deserves rescue. No mention of any righteousness is made. It seems to be Abraham's righteousness that effects rescue, a righteousness perhaps exhibited in the prayer in which Abraham dares to stand as YHWH's bargaining partner and equal.

The memory of the destruction of Sodom lingers in biblical horizon; it lingers because prayer that moves into and against the disorder of the world in passionate intercession is perhaps the deepest, most dangerous, and most compelling prayer in biblical faith. We may mention three uses that derive from this remarkable prayer:

First, in prophetic tradition, Jerusalem is condemned as "not unlike Sodom" in its evil (Isa. 1:10; Jer. 23:14), a theme continued in the New Testament (Matt. 10:15; 11:23–24; Luke 10:12). While there is endless dispute about the nature of Sodom's guilt, Ezekiel situates Sodom (and Jerusalem) in the midst of crass economic failure:

> This was the guilt of your sister Sodom: she and her daughters had pride, excess of food and prosperous ease, but did not aid the poor and needy. They were haughty, and did abominable things before me; therefore I removed them when I saw it. (Ezek. 16:49–50 NRSV)

The way in which the world contradicts the intention of God is persistent, a contradiction that makes prayers of intercession urgent.

Second, in Hosea 11:8–9, YHWH does a radical reversal from intended judgment against Israel. In verse 8, the verb rendered "recoils" is the same Hebrew word as "overthrow" in Genesis 19:25, and Admah and Zeboiim in verse 8 are reckoned as poetic equivalents to Sodom and Gomorrah. Thus this text suggests that God moves abruptly to mercy and so internalizes the "earthquake" so that there will be no further destruction against God's people. The mercy sought by Abraham is not cheap or easy for YHWH, but it is finally enacted!

Third, in Jeremiah 5:1–5, the quest in Jerusalem for "one person who acts justly" is continued. There is seeking among the poor and then among the rich . . . but there is not one! Thus the prayer for "ten" in Genesis 18 is irrelevant in the city that lacks "one."

The prayer of Abraham is a model prayer:

- It features Abraham as the one who takes daring initiative with God with reference to need in the world.
- Abraham moves in on God, instructs God, and warns God about being careless and indiscriminate.
- Abraham practices intercession for the city, not even mentioning his nephew Lot.

The prayer is concerned with big issues—justice and urban destruction—and dares to summon God out beyond God's first inclination. From the beginning, Israel's prayer is bold and focused on justice issues. In YHWH, Abraham finds a "prayer partner" who is competent and ready to be engaged. While that particular prayer of Abraham did not "work," it stands at the beginning of a long history of intercession in which the faithful must hold up their end of "the bargain."

Questions for Reflection and Discussion

1. In what ways is Abraham a positive model for faith?
2. What does it mean to call God "holy"?
3. How should we pray for the salvation of today's cities?

Chapter Two

Moses

Numbers 14:13–23

Moses, the dominant figure in Old Testament faith, is characteristically and everywhere "the man in the middle":

At his birth he was placed in the middle of the river for his survival and protection (Exod. 2:3–4). Well, he was at the edge of the river and not in the middle, but in the middle between the banks of the river, a relatively safe place.

When he was grown, he found himself in the middle between a brutalizing Egyptian taskmaster and a Hebrew slave (Exod. 2:11–15). In that narrative he is caught between his old Egyptian connection (see Exod. 2:10) and the cause of "his people" and their "forced labor" (2:11). There is no doubt that this violent confrontation compelled him into his vocation as the liberator of Israel and as the disturber of the Egyptian empire and its cheap labor policies.

In much larger scope, the central drama of the Exodus narrative is that Moses is cast between YHWH and Pharaoh. Indeed, YHWH clearly authorizes and dispatches Moses to Pharaoh:

So come, I will send you to Pharaoh to bring my people, the Israelites, out of Egypt. (Exod. 3:10 NRSV)

The series of confrontations between YHWH and Pharaoh feature Moses in a contest with the "Egyptian magicians" (research

11

and development guys) to determine whose "magic" would prevail (Exod. 5–11). Moses is repeatedly YHWH's messenger who must go to Pharaoh with a messenger formula, "Thus says YHWH . . ." Moses must deliver a word that is other than his own, a word that seeks to threaten, subvert, and delegitimate the mighty empire; it is, consequently, no surprise that the word mediated to Pharaoh is an unwelcome word that is every time resisted and rejected.

Eventually Moses is situated by the narrative in the middle between YHWH and Israel. On the one hand, he is compelled by YHWH into risky venture on behalf of Israel; on the other hand, Israel is regularly resistant and skeptical about his leadership. Moses had anticipated such resistance, for, at the very outset, he responded to YHWH's summons:

> But suppose they do not believe me or listen to me, but say, "The Lord did not appear to you." (Exod. 4:1 NRSV).

YHWH's assurance to Moses is to guarantee miracles that will attest to Moses' legitimacy and to YHWH's faithful power.

Already in the Exodus narrative itself, and before the Israelites ever leave Egypt, Israel resists Moses' leadership and accuses him of putting them at risk:

> They said to Moses, "Was it because there were no graves in Egypt that you have taken us away to die in the wilderness? What have you done to us, bringing us out of Egypt? Is this not the very thing we told you in Egypt, 'Let us alone and let us serve the Egyptians'? For it would have been better for us to serve the Egyptians than to die in the wilderness." But Moses said to the people, "Do not be afraid, stand firm, and see the deliverance that the Lord will accomplish for you today; for the Egyptians whom you see today you shall never see again. (Exod. 14:11–13 NRSV)

And in the sojourn from Egypt to Sinai, Moses continues to be at odds with Israel, for the divine resolve is not persuasive to anxious slaves on their way to a new life:

The Israelites said to them, "If only we had died by the hand of the Lord in the land of Egypt, when we sat by the flesh-pots and ate our fill of bread; for you have brought us out into this wilderness to kill this whole assembly with hunger." (Exod. 16:3 NRSV)

The people quarreled with Moses, and said, "Give us water to drink." Moses said to them, "Why do you quarrel with me? Why do you test the Lord?" But the people thirsted there for water; and the people complained against Moses and said, "Why did you bring us out of Egypt, to kill us and our children and livestock with thirst?" (Exod. 17:2–3 NRSV)

In response to such resistance, Moses in exasperation seeks guidance from YHWH, and receives an assurance:

So Moses cried out to the Lord, "What shall I do with this people? They are almost ready to stone me." The Lord said to Moses, "Go on ahead of the people, and take some of the elders of Israel with you; take in your hand the staff with which you struck the Nile, and go. I will be standing there in front of you on the rock at Horeb. Strike the rock, and water will come out of it, so that the people may drink." Moses did so, in the sight of the elders of Israel. (Exod. 17:4–6 NRSV)

As it was in Egypt (14:11–13) and on the initial sojourn toward Sinai (Exod. 16–17), so it continued at Sinai. In the narrative of Exodus 32–34, YHWH is in dispute with Israel in the form of Aaron, the producer of the golden calf. In order to fend off YHWH's anger against "stiff-necked" Israel, Moses prays that YHWH should "change your mind" on the basis of YHWH's promise to the Genesis ancestors (Exod. 32:12–13). Finally, in order to begin again in covenant after the breach caused by Aaron and the breaking of the tablets of the commandments (Exod. 32:19), YHWH and Moses have a vigorous exchange in which YHWH asserts YHWH's gracious freedom (Exod. 33:19).

YHWH then makes a self-announcement concerning both YHWH's fidelity and YHWH's starchy rigor:

> The Lord passed before him, and proclaimed,
> "The Lord, the Lord,
> a God merciful and gracious,
> slow to anger,
> and abounding in steadfast love and faithfulness,
> keeping steadfast love for the thousandth generation,
> forgiving iniquity and transgression and sin,
> yet by no means clearing the guilty,
> but visiting the iniquity of the parents
> upon the children
> and the children's children,
> to the third and the fourth generation."
>   (Exod. 34:6–7 NRSV)

In response to the self-announcement, Moses prays that YHWH may "pardon" Israel (Exod. 34:8–9) and YHWH agrees to renew the covenant (Exod. 34:10). The interaction between YHWH and Moses evidences a deep practice of prayer in which he must intervene vigorously with YHWH on behalf of wayward Israel. Moses' prayer is answered and life begins again between the covenant partners. The man "in the middle" has revived the covenant through his daring intervention!

As the narrative carries Israel from the contested encounter at Sinai to the wilderness sojourn, matters do not improve between the two parties. The wilderness is found to be an arena of scant resources for life, so scant that Israel is angry, Moses is displeased, and YHWH in turn is provoked to acute anger against complaining Israel. YHWH and Israel are in fact fed up with each other, and Moses is, yet again, caught between them. In Numbers 14, the chapter offering the prayer that we consider, Israel again wants to escape the wilderness, revoke the Exodus, and find alternative leadership to head back into Egyptian slavery:

So they said to one another, "Let us choose a captain, and go back to Egypt." (Num. 14:4 NRSV)

The proposal is a repudiation of the leadership of Moses and the intention of YHWH. Given such a persistent "murmur," YHWH is exasperated and shares that exasperation with Moses, YHWH's singular confidant. YHWH begins his reaction to Israelite complaint with a double "How long?"—a recurring phrase of exhausted patience:

And the Lord said to Moses, "How long will this people despise me? And how long will they refuse to believe in me, in spite of all the signs that I have done among them?" (Num. 14:11 NRSV)

After YHWH's complaint about Israel to Moses, YHWH issues to Moses a remarkable alternative proposal that YHWH should eliminate Israel, which is much too recalcitrant, and form a new nation only from Moses:

I will strike them with pestilence and disinherit them, and I will make of you a nation greater and mightier than they. (Num. 14:12 NRSV)

That is, YHWH seeks to "triangle" . . . YHWH-with-Moses . . . against Israel which is to be excluded from the future. YHWH will find in Moses a partner who is adequate, who in fidelity is unlike Israel. But Moses will have none of the triangling and, in the end, cares more for Israel than does YHWH. It is this uncommon commitment of Moses to Israel that evokes the prayer that follows. Out of devotion to Israel, Moses resists YHWH's alternative plan that entailed the termination of Israel.

In verses 13–19 Moses addresses YHWH in one of the great prayers of the Bible. The prayer turns on the petition of verse 17, but before the petition can be voiced, verses 13–16, in two parts, provide a context and setup for the petition. The first part of the setup concerns the risk to YHWH that the Egyptians will hear of the termination of Israel and will misconstrue that savage ending wrought by YHWH's abandonment of Israel (vv. 13–14). Worse yet, the Egyptians will report the termination of Israel to Israel's more immediate threat, the inhabitants of the land of Canaan. YHWH had decisively defeated Pharaoh (Exod. 15:1–8), but now YHWH will be perceived as a failure, thus granting to Pharaoh a belated (posthumous?) final victory. The Egyptians and the "Canaanites" know that YHWH's power is fully committed to Israel and will, consequently, conclude that YHWH's power is unreliable and lacks the capacity to follow through.

The second part of the setup parallels the Egyptians to "the nations who have heard of you" (Num. 14:15–16a). The phrase refers to all those whom Israel must meet along the way to the land of promise, or perhaps alludes to the classic list of "seven nations" that became stereotypical in the tradition (see Deut. 7:1–2). The reference is not specific but refers to all those who have resisted Israel and doubted YHWH. The key phrase is the mistaken judgment that outsiders will make that YHWH is "not able" and therefore Israel is terminated. The nations cannot imagine that YHWH has "character" enough to grow impatient with Israel and will not tolerate Israel's endless complaints that are an affront to the majesty of YHWH. They do not know that YHWH trades in covenantal transactions and requires and expects responsiveness; they presume that YHWH, like every other god they know, operates only in terms of power. And they will conclude, given such a category mistake, that YHWH's power has failed.

The import of the warning to YHWH concerning Egypt, the inhabitants of the land, and the nations who have heard is that they are all watching and waiting to see whether YHWH can fulfill his oath of deliverance . . . or if YHWH's power and resolve will fail. The nations watch and hope that YHWH's initial resolve on behalf of Israel is an empty one, for if it is an empty one, then the status quo among the nations can remain undisturbed. The spectacular assumption of the entire utterance of Moses to YHWH is that YHWH is self-consciously concerned about the judgment the other nations will make. That is, YHWH is vain enough to care about such "world opinion," that such a judgment made on YHWH will amount to a loss of face in the conflicted world where YHWH must compete for a valid reputation. To be sure, such an address to YHWH that warns YHWH of bad consequences of a decision made in impatient anger strikes us as theologically ignoble.

But such is the nature of prayer in the Bible, and such is the nature of regressive, desperate prayer among us when we are pressed to appeal to God's self-interest. More than that, before we are repelled by Moses' strategic utterance, we may take note of the quite familiar enterprise of praise in which worship regularly consists. Taken at its most elemental level, praise addressed to God is not done so that the singer may feel better, but so that God may be enhanced and magnified—made bigger—in the eyes of the community, among outsiders to the community, and among the other gods. Moses appeals to God's self-maintenance and self-care, for Moses knows that YHWH cares not only for Israel and for the world, but for God's own self. Moses can anticipate, more than can YHWH in YHWH's indignation, the unwanted consequences of the decision YHWH is about to make in anger.

With the completion of his warning to YHWH, Moses makes the rhetorical transition to the petition toward which the prayer has been moving: "And now therefore . . ." (v. 17). It is as though YHWH awaits a better idea, better than disastrous anger. Moses' petition offers just such a "better idea." He proposes, instead of massive destruction that terminates Israel and that may satisfy momentarily YHWH's raw sensibility, that YHWH should make an exhibit of great positive power. Moses refers to the constructive power of fidelity to which YHWH had previously committed when YHWH remade the broken covenant with Israel in the narrative of the golden calf (Exod. 34:10). All parties have known since that crisis that continuation with YHWH after the break of the covenant depends solely upon YHWH's faithful forbearance and resolve. This present crisis in the wilderness is a replica of that remembered crisis at Sinai.

And then, in a remarkable act of textual reference, Moses quotes YHWH's own words from Exodus 34:6–7 back to YHWH:

> The Lord passed before him, and proclaimed,
>> "The Lord, the Lord,
>> a God merciful and gracious,
>> slow to anger,
>> and abounding in steadfast love and faithfulness,
>> keeping steadfast love for the thousandth generation,
>> forgiving iniquity and transgression and sin,
>> yet by no means clearing the guilty,
>> but visiting the iniquity of the parents
>> upon the children
>> and the children's children,
>> to the third and the fourth generation."
>> (Exod. 34:6–7 NRSV)

> The Lord is slow to anger,
> and abounding in steadfast love,
> forgiving iniquity and transgression,
> but by no means clearing the guilty,
> visiting the iniquity of the parents
> upon the children
> to the third and the fourth generation.
> (Num. 14:18 NRSV)

Moses prays back to YHWH using YHWH's own self-characterization; in reiterating that self-announcement, Moses reminds YHWH of who YHWH has resolved to be, and summons YHWH back to YHWH's own self-resolve. In substance the petition of verses 17–18 addressed to YHWH is, "Be your true self!" It is as though YHWH, in great indignation in verses 11–12, had regressed enough to forget and disregard YHWH's "best self." That best self is characterized by *immense fidelity*. The prayer and the text behind it employ words that characterize YHWH's steadfast, abiding, trustworthy commitment . . . "slow to anger . . . steadfast love, forgiving." (The original in Exodus 34:6–7 had even more such language, not all of which is repeated here, but all of which is surely implied and understood by all parties.) The quote from YHWH's own lips acknowledges that punishment is legitimate and appropriate, but surely urges that such a reaction as YHWH has proposed in verse 12 is not appropriate. It is clear that in this prayer Moses remembers what YHWH has forgotten about YHWH's own self-resolve.

On the basis of that textual reminder, Moses, in verse 19, issues the big imperative: Pardon! The basis of the proposed pardon is YHWH's steadfast love. There is no thought that Israel deserves pardon or that YHWH is obligated to forgive. It is, rather, that YHWH's steadfast love, YHWH's most core identity, binds YHWH to Israel in spite of all transgressive disobedience and rejection on the part of Israel. This is indeed an appeal to God's grace that is rooted in nothing more than the claim that YHWH is gracious. Moses, moreover, asserts that YHWH has been in the practice of pardoning Israel ever since the exodus, certainly in the great crisis of Sinai (Exod. 32–34), and in many wilderness encounters. It is in the nature of this covenantal relationship that its continuation depends upon YHWH's readiness to pardon. The prayer asks that YHWH should do YHWH's most transformative act one more time. Thus the appeal concerns YHWH's character. But Moses' negative warning in verses 13–16 adds the additional argument that it is in YHWH's own self-interest to act according to YHWH's character.

The prayer of Moses (vv. 13–19) evokes a vigorous, complex response from YHWH, who answers prayer but answers in YHWH's own freedom (vv. 20–23). The divine response is in three parts. First, YHWH concedes the main point to Moses. YHWH will pardon, just as Moses had petitioned (v. 20). YHWH accepts the point and acknowledges YHWH's own true character. The crisis thus could be seen as resolved.

Except that second, YHWH immediately severely qualifies the generous assurance of verse 20 (vv. 21–23). The qualification of the "assurance of pardon" is terse: "Nevertheless!" YHWH asserts YHWH's glory, that is, the splendor of YHWH's sovereign majesty that will overwhelm all the earth. The nature of YHWH's glory is elusive, but here it would seem to be in some tension with YHWH's steadfast love (see Exod. 33:18–20). If YHWH's *steadfast love*—the basis of Moses' petition—is for the sake of Israel, then the *glory* is for the sake of YHWH, the exhibit of YHWH before the watching nations. In his petition Moses had connected YHWH's "great power" (v. 17) to "steadfast love" (v. 18), but here they fall apart. Instead, YHWH speaks and resolves to punish harshly the ones who did not listen; it is a central conviction of the Old Testament tradition that the faithless generation of the wilderness will not complete the trek to the land of promise. There must be a deep caesura between the older generation of disobedience and the new generation that will receive the land. It is not easy to see what the "pardon" of verse 20 might mean in light of the divine resolve of verses 21–23. It is as though YHWH pays lip service to the petition of Moses, but then disregards it in self-exhibiting resolve. The news is not good and the petition would seem to have failed.

Except, third, YHWH provides that Caleb—only Caleb of the older generation—will receive the promise. He is the embodiment of continuity from the older generation to the newer generation (as Dennis Olson has shown; in much of the tradition it is Caleb and Joshua, but Joshua is not mentioned here; see Num. 14:6, 30; 26:65; 32:12). Caleb is "different." He obeys fully. The one who qualifies is the one with a responsive spirit, ready to hear and obey. Thus the survival of Caleb is the assurance that YHWH will not terminate Israel as previously proposed. It is curious, nonetheless, that the resolve to sustain Caleb is not grounded in YHWH's steadfast love, but in Caleb's adherence to YHWH's command. Thus YHWH pardons, but the pardon does not go very far in exhibiting what Moses has proposed, *great power as deep steadfast love*. YHWH does not appear here to measure up to the deep hope and urgent insistence of Moses. The prayer has impacted YHWH, but only partially and guardedly.

Moses is a powerful man of prayer, and a compelling model of prayer. His prayer suggests:

- That bold prayer is to stand in "the breach," hopefully to be a "repairer of the breach" between God and God's people or God and God's world (see Isa. 58:12). Such a position is one of daring and of exposure, for it assumes that God can be, and is indeed, impacted by such prayer.
- That bold prayer is evoked by a love of the community (church or world) and that such love evokes a crisis with God and invites a confrontation. It is evident in this exchange that Moses loves Israel more passionately than does YHWH, and it is this greater passion that sets the tone of urgency in the prayer.
- That greater passion prods Moses to take an initiative with God that pushes beyond God's own intentionality. In such prayer it is clear that God does not take all initiatives, as may be the case in much conventional theology. Moses invites God into the unexplored territory of forgiveness and pardon.
- That such prayer grows out of a long, trusting history of interaction. Moses does not come before YHWH as a stranger with a new idea, but prays out of a long history as an old and well-established colleague and confidant of YHWH.
- That prayer is not conjured on the spot out of emotional need, nor is it completely spontaneous. Moses, in his prayer, is deeply rooted in textual tradition and had spent time studying what was to become Scripture. There is no doubt that the Scripture he quotes, Exodus 34:6–7, is taken to be God's own utterance; thus Moses is able, because he knows the textual tradition, to pray the text back to God, and to call God to account.

- That such prayer is between friends, rooted in history, and grounded in a textual tradition. Given all of that, Moses nonetheless knows that he must take into account YHWH's own self-regard. That is why Moses can warn about pending mistaken reactions of other peoples. In a lesser agent, one might think that appeal to YHWH's self-regard is to play upon YHWH's vanity. And indeed one may conclude that YHWH is vain and cares about other peoples' opinions too much. If, however, our view of God is too high and noble for such a judgment, then we may leave it as legitimate self-regard and not as vanity.
- That in such prayer, Moses (and Israel) must engage the endlessly tricky issue of *divine power* and *divine fidelity*. There is no doubt that power is a governing quality of all gods, in the ancient world as in the contemporary world. Fidelity, however, is another matter, the one to which Moses appeals. It would appear that YHWH concedes something to the Mosaic accent on fidelity, but the self-reference of God concerning "the glory of the Lord" indicates that the exhibit of divine majesty crowds out some consideration of fidelity. It is clear that in prayer Moses must take into account not only the risk and need of Israel but the character of God as well. That is, prayer requires us to be knowingly and intentionally *theological*, because it is to *God* that we pray.

In the end, the proposal of Moses and the resolution wrought by YHWH are all "for God's sake." The benefit to Israel is a by-product, but the refusal on YHWH's part to be more generous is because YHWH has not been "heard" and insists upon being heard. It belongs to God to be heard; it belongs to Israel to hear, to obey, and to follow. Caleb is an exemplar of faithful Israel. It is to him that the future belongs. With that much settled for now, YHWH can instruct Moses in the next steps toward the fulfillment of the promise, a promise to be received only by those with "a different spirit" (v. 25).

Questions for Reflection and Discussion

1. How do we share our exasperation in prayers to God?
2. How can we pray for God's self-interest?
3. Where should we stand "in the middle" like Moses?

Chapter Three

Hannah

1 Samuel 2:1–10

Israel's prayer is mostly "asking," petitions that seek YHWH's intervention in situations of need and abandonment and help-lessness. As we have seen, Israel's petitions sometimes run to intercession for others, as when Abraham prays for the well-being of Sodom and Moses prays for the forgiveness of Israel. Israel's prayers are sometimes answered. YHWH responds with gener-ous gifts and astonishing reversals that break cycles of need, end seasons of abandonment, overcome situations of helplessness, and put Israel on a whole new course for life.

When Israel experiences such wondrous gifts from YHWH, its prayers perforce must change. In such contexts, Israel's prayers turn to joy, celebration, thanksgiving, and praise. Israel is left astonished and dazzled by YHWH's gift of newness and abandons itself in response to YHWH in unqualified exuberance. Gifts from YHWH given to Israel are characteristically beyond anticipation or explanation. The only appropriate response is glad self-aban-donment that acknowledges YHWH as the giver of all good gifts.

The "Song of Hannah" in 1 Samuel 2:1–10 is just such a prayer of exuberant celebration. Before the prayer was situated (through editorial process) in the book of Samuel, it is likely that it was an independent liturgical piece that could have been used in a differ-ent context before being placed in its present narrative context.

24

There is no compelling necessity that the prayer must be on the lips of Hannah, for this prayer is properly on the lips of Israel. The prayer is a celebration of a newly given king ("anointed," verse 10), and so may be best situated in the Jerusalem liturgy where the Davidic king is celebrated. The Davidic king is acknowledged as a gift from YHWH, a human agent authorized and empowered to do YHWH's transformative, revolutionary, justice-bringing work in the earth. The poem is framed in verses 1 and 10 by the Hebrew "horn" (rendered as "strength"), bespeaking the virile capacity of the human king. The two uses together form a rhetorical envelope for the whole in which human strength is recognized and acknowledged to be a gift from YHWH.

In verse 1 the speaker, perhaps Israel, perhaps the king, eventually Hannah, celebrates YHWH in exuberant ways for empowerment from YHWH that gives leverage over enemies and assures victory. These verses are dominated by the first-person pronoun "my," but it is clear that everything claimed for and by the speaker is from YHWH. It is because of YHWH that the speaker is empowered and emboldened in a context of deep conflict. One may imagine the king boasting about a victory over enemies, or Israel celebrating such a victory, all with reference to YHWH.

In verses 2–8, the poem moves from human boasting to praise of YHWH, who is the ground of human boasting (see Jer. 9:22–23 on proper boasting with reference to YHWH). Verse 2 asserts a "formula of incomparability," an oft-repeated liturgical claim that YHWH is unique in power and in compassion, and cannot be compared to any other god. Thus Israel at prayer voices complete confidence in YHWH's reliability and holiness, which are so overwhelming that they are sure to silence any pride or boasting arrogance on the part of adversaries, the ones mentioned in verse 1. YHWH is so awesome and impressive—in the doxological horizon of Israel—that all other rivals are shown by contrast to be weak, feeble, and inconsequential. Thus the self-confidence of verse 1 and confidence in YHWH in verse 2 are of a piece. Praise yields boasting confidence; the act of praise is a process of gathering the vigor and courage of king and community.

The poem turns in predictable doxological fashion in verse 3 with the pivotal preposition "for" which introduces the reasons for Israel's exuberant confidence. Israel's prayer of praise is saturated with such "reasons" that consist in a recital of YHWH's actions and YHWH's attributes. All of verses 3b–8 are governed by this "for," and constitute an inventory of the wonders of YHWH that evoke and merit self-abandoning praise.

The reasons for praise of YHWH are offered in three clusters:

(a) In verse 3b, YHWH is acknowledged as the all-knowing, all-judging God of creation (see Isa. 40:21–23). Nothing appears or happens that is beyond the purview and adjudication of YHWH.

(b) In verses 4–5 the claim of verse 3b is made specific. What is precisely under the surveillance of YHWH is the social imbalance

- between *the mighty and the feeble,*
- between *the full and the hungry,*
- between *the fruitful and the barren.*

In the usual scheme of things the mighty, the full, and the fruitful are dominant, and their dominance is taken as normal. But YHWH sees! YHWH notices, and in that notice there is recognition that such inequity and consequent exploitation is abnormal and cannot stand. This vast awareness of YHWH keeps what the world regards as normal under severe scrutiny. These verses not only describe; they notice and anticipate that the abnormality of inequity will be corrected. In these verses, rhetoric is no doubt utilized to speak of YHWH's active intervention. The verbs are passive, but the inference is clear. The abnormality is to be overcome because YHWH weighs and governs toward better outcomes. The world is being reordered according to the resolve and reality of YHWH.

It is important to notice that YHWH's hidden (providential) resolve concerns the most concrete social realities. It is this God who designs the world on behalf of the feeble. The "strength" to be given to the feeble may refer back to the "strength" celebrated in verse 1, even though the terms are different. The second word pair of "full-hungry" speaks of the distribution of food. And the third word pair, "fruitful-barren" speaks of social stability and perhaps even health care. Those who are strong and full prosper with "many." Those who are feeble and hungry have little future into the next generation. All of this that the world accepts so readily will not stand, because YHWH sees, knows, and wills otherwise, albeit in hidden ways that require passive verbs. The prayer has confidence that the world eventually will be the world intended by YHWH, a world contradicted by present unjust power arrangements!

(c) What is stated hiddenly—in passive verbs—in verses 4–5 is, in verses 6–8b, now made explicit with active verbs. In these lines of the prayer YHWH is the subject of the verbs and agent of radical transformative action. YHWH is named twice, echoing the name of YHWH in verses 1 and 3. It is central to Israel's doxological prayer that YHWH is portrayed and attested as an active agent. In this doxological sensibility, Israel gives no explanation for how divine agency is affected, nor does Israel exhibit any trouble with or curiosity about such a question. Doxological prayer is as direct and confident as Israel's petitionary prayer is direct and insistent. The God from whom intervention is sought is the God celebrated for interventions already known and those still anticipated.

Verse 6 makes the most sweeping claim: "kills-gives life," "brings down-raises up." The word pairs attest to YHWH's complete, unlimited power over all the processes of creation, life and death. The singular sweeping claim made here is echoed in the later text of Isaiah 45:7, which is on its way to monotheism:

> I form light and create darkness,
> I make weal and create woe;
> I the Lord do all these things.
> (Isa. 45:7)

The verbs surely suggest that YHWH is capable of incredible and unchecked violence; the intent, however, is not to celebrate divine violence, but to submit the world to YHWH, A to Z. There is none who has life without YHWH; there is no other who can eliminate life (see Rom. 14:7–8). The mood of the utterance is doxological, intending in the most imaginative way possible to credit all to the God who is the subject of Israel's praise.

This remarkable claim for YHWH's administration of the processes of creation is brought closer to concrete social reality in the verses that follow. Israel has little speculative interest in the dead or in the later claim of resurrection. Rather, Israel's horizon here is fixed on social inequity and the possibility of worldly redress. The focal subject of verses 7–8a are "rich and poor," a social pair correlated with those "brought down" and those "raised up." The "rich-poor" pair summarizes the three word pairs of verses 4–5: mighty-feeble, full-hungry, and fruitful-barren. After the contrasting pair in verse 7, the prayer moves to its proper subject in verse 8, the poor and the needy. This prayer knows about the environment of those disadvantaged who are powerless, helpless, and without resources. The poor and the needy are regularly diminished, humiliated, and degraded; for them the "ash heap" stands as a proper metaphor. The anticipation of the prayer, however, is that the helpless will not long remain in such a state, because the God who weighs and sees and knows will not leave the poor and weak permanently disadvantaged. Thus the prayer imagines, anticipates, and already knows about radical social transformation. The poor and the needy will occupy places of honor, power, and dignity alongside princes. The throne will be crowded and the royals will need to move over a little to share space. The prayer imagines the ending of normal arrangements to make way for the alternative arrangements of the God who holds all of life and death in divine hands. The world will change! The world will not and cannot stay as it is!

The final lines of verse 8 seal the deal by pushing behind and below social reality to cosmic foundations. The world, in ancient imagination, sits on pillars that reach to the bottom of thinkable reality. It is YHWH who has made it so. YHWH is the owner and manager of those foundations. This doxological acclamation thus has a parallel to the opening claim of verses 2–3. Social reality in verses 4–8a is bracketed by the claims made for the creator. The scope of creation forms the arena for YHWH's saving activity. But it is all of a piece. The creator intends social power to be reorganized. The creator is peculiarly allied with the poor, the needy, the feeble, the hungry, and the barren (see Prov. 17:5). When the creator God acts for those allies, the princes may expect to be squeezed and crowded by the new arrangement. Room must be made for the newly esteemed!

The poem veers sharply in a new direction in the rhetoric of verse 9. YHWH is still the subject of the powerful verbs. But now the contrasts of social inequity are transposed into terms concerning those who keep covenant and those who do not. The contrast is between "the faithful" and "the wicked." It is the faithful, those allied with YHWH, who will be kept safely. Verse 10 lines out the way in which YHWH will *guard* on the one hand and *cut off* on the other hand, a contrast that reflects Israel's most elemental conviction, reflected in Psalm 1 and Deuteronomy 30:15–20.

In verse 10, the prayer articulates a familiar but nonetheless stunning juxtaposition that characterizes Israel's faith. On the one hand, the first three lines of the verse celebrate YHWH in extravagant doxological language. The verse begins with an abrupt articulation of the divine name of YHWH. The name stands alone in the line, uninflected. But the implication is enormous. YHWH's adversaries, the "wicked" of verse 9, are to be "brought low." In these lines, the divine name is given in a sequence of three: YHWH, Most High, and YHWH. The one praised is the cosmic judge, the mighty creator who will prevail, to the benefit of the faithful. It is all YHWH, only YHWH!

But then on the other hand, in the last lines of the verse, the rhetoric turns from YHWH the Most High to "his king, his anointed." It is the human king, the Davidic king, who is empowered now to do the work of YHWH in guarding the faithful and cutting off the wicked. The juxtaposition of *the Most High* and *the Davidic king* is an essential of Israel's faith, for Israel regularly assigns all large acts of transformation to YHWH and then anticipates that human agents will effect divine purpose. Israel refuses to choose, either that it is all divine action or all human achievement. It is divine action via human agent. In much traditional Christian piety, prayer is a form of abdication of human responsibility by the expectation that God will act. But not here. Here, as is usual in the Old Testament, it is YHWH through human agency. Thus for example in Exodus 3:7–10, YHWH resolves to act but then sends Moses. In Judges 5:11 the "triumphs" are the "triumphs of YHWH," but in the next line they are the "triumphs of his peasants." Israel's prayer anticipates that YHWH's divine action is accomplished through designated human agents—in the case of this prayer, the agency of David, the one anointed.

If we take this insight from verse 10 and read it back into the prayer, we can see that the enormous doxological vigor concerning YHWH's revolutionary action may be understood at the same time as buoyancy about human possibility that is made possible by YHWH's strong, bold empowerment of human leadership. The prayer is not an abdication but an expectation and an acceptance of human responsibility that is doxologically rooted.

We may imagine that this great utterance of hope and new worldly possibility was used and continues to echo in a variety of contexts.

1. The focus on royal strength and revolutionary social vision suggests that the prayer is a royal psalm that was utilized to celebrate and legitimate the Davidic monarchy. Thus its liturgic habitat may have been the Jerusalem temple. If that is so, then the prayer, in early usage, may have functioned like Psalm 72, a royal psalm that assigns to the royal office the task of justice for the poor and the needy:

> For he delivers *the needy* when they call,
>   *the poor* and those who have no helper.
> He has pity on *the weak* and *the needy*,
>   and saves the lives of *the needy*.
> From oppression and violence he redeems their life;
>   and precious is their blood in his sight.
>   (Ps. 72:12–14 NRSV; see vv. 1–4).

That liturgical usage may be supported by a recognition that Psalm 113:5–9, also a liturgic piece, voices the same revolutionary expectation. In that psalm there is no mention of a human king; revolutionary newness is credited directly to YHWH who is "seated on high." But the juxtaposition of Psalms 72 and 113 reflects the tense interface of *divine resolve* and *human agency* that is everywhere in Old Testament faith.

2. As we now have the prayer of Hannah, it is situated in the narrative of 1 Samuel. The placement of the prayer in the narrative changes the intent and impact of the prayer. Now the issue concerns not liturgical imagination, but the question of how to begin the narrative of kingship in ancient Israel. It is clear in Judges 17–21, the text that precedes 1 Samuel, that the old social order has failed. The narrator wants to give an account of a new royal possibility that will culminate in the wonder of David and the splendor of Solomon. But how to begin?

The chosen strategy for telling this story is to begin where Israel's story often begins, with a barren mother who has no son and so a people that has no future (see Gen. 11:30). In this instance, it is Hannah who is barren and who prays in her desperate status. In a way that is not explained, her prayer is heard! She is pregnant and is given a son:

> They rose early in the morning and worshiped before the Lord; then they went back to their house at Ramah. Elkanah knew his wife Hannah, and the Lord remembered her. In due time Hannah conceived and bore a son. She named him Samuel, for she said, "I have asked him of the Lord." (1 Sam. 1:19–20 NRSV)

Hannah knows that the new baby is a gift from YHWH. She knows that the new baby must be given over to the purposes of YHWH . . . and the narrator knows that those purposes have to do with David, who is to come soon into the narrative (see 1 Sam. 16:1–13). This barren woman becomes a mother who must sing! A song that was about a king coming to victory is now about a mother who comes to joy. The birth of the son is a sign of much that is to come by the generosity of YHWH. But before little Samuel is taken as a large sign of public faith, he is to be taken as a little baby given as a miracle in response to a needy, tearful prayer of a woman without resources. YHWH has answered prayer!

The answer is this precious baby who will open the family of Elkanah to newness and open the people Israel to a royal future. It takes the narrative only one chapter to arrive at a wondrous verdict:

> Now the boy Samuel continued to grow both in stature and in favor with the Lord and with the people. (1 Sam. 2:26 NRSV)

And it takes only one more chapter beyond that to bring the boy Samuel to significant adulthood as the carrier of YHWH's word in Israel, an adult soon to be a kingmaker:

> As Samuel grew up, the Lord was with him and let none of his words fall to the ground. And all Israel from Dan to Beer-sheba knew that Samuel was a trustworthy prophet of the Lord. The Lord continued to appear at Shiloh, for the Lord revealed himself to Samuel at Shiloh by the word of the Lord. (1 Sam. 3:19–21 NRSV)

No wonder Hannah could sing! She sings of a surprise in gratitude. She sings that her family will continue. She sings that her people will have a future. She sings that through this little baby named "asked" there will soon be newness for the poor and needy and hungry and feeble. She sings in the way singing is possible only among those who have felt the powerful invasiveness of YHWH's newness where no newness was possible. She sings of the God who "brings life." She sings of the God who raises up. This is the God who lifts the needy. Hannah is the voice of all those who still have ashes in their hair and in their throats, who find themselves on the way to royal banquets and safe places . . . all this,

- accomplished by the God who is Most High,
- accomplished by the anointed who will have power,
- accomplished by this son for whom she had not dared to hope . . . but only prayed!

There was a king in the liturgy who expected victory. But then there was a mother who found speech at wondrous birth. And finally there was a writer who understood that history begins again by divine mystery; it is this God who presides over the rise and the fall of great powers. In this moment, it is the "rise" that is to be celebrated in Israel, even though this same historian, before the narrative is finished, must tell of the "fall" of YHWH's people and YHWH's city (see 2 Kgs. 24–25).

3. It is not any surprise that the church, in its celebrative wonder about Jesus, could appropriate the Song of Hannah, even as the narrator had appropriated Psalm 113 from the liturgy. The New Testament can take up this same prayer, though the appropriation of the church is not a monopoly, and Jews can continue to sing the song even as Christians sing it as their own.

In the New Testament and in Christian liturgical usage, the Song of Hannah has been transposed into the Song of Mary, the Magnificat in Luke 1:46–55. Luke had the same problem as did the historian of David's rise to power. How to begin the story? Luke does not begin that story in the same way as did Matthew, Mark, or John. Luke begins with a woman without a baby. Mary is not barren, but a virgin. But she, like Hannah, is given a baby she did not expect. She willingly accepted her role as his mother (Luke 1:38). And she must sing! After her song, as we say, the rest is history!

Mary sang of the baby born wondrously, and then focuses upon the God who gives the baby. The "Mighty One" is holy, but filled with mercy (Luke 1:49). That divine mercy, moreover, is now embodied in this baby Jesus, mercy that continues to work revolution in the world. It is a revolution to which the narrative of Luke is fully committed. In the Song of Mary, the revolution echoes the lyric of Hannah's song:

> He has brought down the powerful from their thrones,
>   and lifted up the lowly;
> he has filled the hungry with good things,
>   and sent the rich away empty.
>   (Luke 1:52–53 NRSV)

The song yet again concerns the lowly and the hungry. In Luke's purview, moreover, the revolution triggered by the song continues in the narrative of Jesus (see Luke 7:22). It is in Luke, with more emphasis than in other accounts, that society is inverted and transformed. The outsiders are welcomed to the banquet (Luke 14:15–24). The prodigal son is welcomed home (Luke 15:11–31). The tax collector is given salvation (Luke 19:1–10). And the story continues as the story of the church . . . rooted in the same song. In the book of Acts, the continuation of Luke's narrative, Christians "turned the world upside down" (Acts 17:6). Mary anticipated the turn of the world; Hannah anticipated the turn of the destiny of Israel. The Jerusalem liturgy before Hannah and before Mary had anticipated the turn of the world. Jerusalem liturgy . . . Hannah . . . Mary . . . the church . . . they all sang!

Hannah must sing. And Mary must sing. And Israel must sing. And the church must sing. We must sing exuberant, self-abandoning doxologies because we have received more than we expected, and we have expected even more than we dared to hope. We imagine that the One who created the world for life will not finish until the world is brought to full, abundant life.

Such an act of praise puts a praying people into a zone of wonder, astonishment, and expectation. It is a wonder that the world can and will be changed toward life. It is an astonishment that the world can and will be changed beyond our explanatory categories. It is an expectation that human agents may participate in divinely willed social transformation. Such exuberant praise does not deliver faithful people from the high risk of daring testimony or from the deep, intractable contradictions of lived reality. In the midst of high risks and intractable contradictions, however, songs of praise, rooted in nameable miracles, provide buoyancy and keep the world open. Every time it enters this zone of doxological amazement, the church echoes the cadences of Hannah. She holds this little baby and imagines a people of faith come of age. She holds this little baby and anticipates a new ordering of the world!

Questions for Reflection and Discussion

1. What prayers of thanksgiving do we pray?
2. Who are the "feeble" ones for whom we should pray?
3. How can we turn our prayers into songs of wonder and astonishment?

Chapter Four

David

2 Samuel 7:18–29

David has been on the way to the throne of Israel since the very beginning.

Even before he was on the scene, he was anticipated. Hannah sang about him as "the anointed" (1 Sam. 2:10). The narrator anticipates him, knowing that he would displace Saul (1 Sam. 13:13–14; 15:26–29). Abigail knew he would prevail (1 Sam. 25:28). As a very young man, even before he was known by anyone, Samuel had anointed him king, and God's empowering spirit had rushed upon him (1 Sam. 16:13).

As he moved toward kingship, however, it was not as easy as it had promised to be. For the throne was already occupied . . . by Saul. David's rise to power required important and risky confrontations with Saul (1 Sam. 24:20–22; 26:25). Before he could become king, his destiny required several convenient deaths, deaths in which David was not quite obviously implicated: Saul (2 Sam. 1:14–16), Abner (2 Sam. 3:28–29, 35–37), and Ishbaal (2 Sam. 4:11). David came through those deaths unscathed . . . but just barely. The narrator permits us to be suspicious about the convenience of all these deaths that removed all threats to David.

With the removal of such political "inconveniences," David can become king as was long before promised. He became king in Judah as the people anointed him (2 Sam. 2:4). Seven years later he became king of Israel by covenantal agreement (2 Sam. 5:1–5). And then finally, he seized Jerusalem and became a proper king in Jerusalem, in David's own city, in "Royal David's city," a city always known as "the city of David," never as "the city of Israel" (2 Sam. 5:6–12).

David became king, partly by ruthless cunning and careful alliances. He became king partly by wondrously good fortune. But the narrative and the faith of Israel believed that David became king because of divine resolve. It was YHWH's intention that David should be king, and he is made king by YHWH's faithful attentiveness to him. The Lord was indeed with him!

David is ensconced in the newly seized city of Jerusalem. He made that alien city a fitting habitat for YHWH by transporting the old ark of the covenant into the city (2 Sam. 6:1–20). And now he had done it! The new king, chosen by YHWH, was safe in his own city, near to Israel's most treasured religious artifact, the ark, the sign of YHWH's protective presence.

But there is more to come! In the night, YHWH speaks an oracle to Nathan, David's prophet (2 Sam. 7:1–17). What an oracle it is! YHWH first asserts YHWH's own freedom, YHWH's unwillingness to be boxed in by cultic furniture (vv. 5–7). The point of the divine oracle, however, does not concern YHWH's freedom. It concerns, rather, YHWH's abiding commitment to David. The oracle reviews the past presented as a narrative of YHWH's fidelity (vv. 8–9). But then YHWH promises to make "a house" for David, that is, a dynasty, so that David's spectacular achievement as king is to be sustained into the future, well beyond his own lifetime (vv. 11–16). This promise to David is perhaps the most remarkable in all of Scripture. The promise includes the assurance that David's son (Solomon) will build a temple and have a privileged relationship to YHWH (vv. 12–14). Most remarkably, YHWH promises that YHWH will never, under any circumstance or for any reason, remove YHWH's fidelity from the dynasty of David:

> But I will not take my steadfast love from him, as I took it from Saul, whom I put away from before you. Your house and

your kingdom shall be made sure forever before me; your
throne shall be established forever. (2 Sam. 7:15–16 NRSV)

This promise amounts to an unconditional divine commitment
without qualification, reservation, or limit. It is an act of sheer
grace that requires nothing of David or of his family.

I have taken so long with this preliminary narrative and oracle,
because the narrative and oracle provide a context of privileged
relationship to God; it is in the context of and in response to that
oracle of unconditional promise that the prayer of David is
uttered. The question left for David is this: how to pray properly
and appropriately in response to an astonishing guarantee that is
rooted only in YHWH's faithful assurance. It is a persistent question for those who are entitled, privileged, gifted, and guaranteed.
Such a status before God requires a specific practice of prayer.

The first thing that strikes one about the rhetoric of David's
prayer is that it is overloaded with generous acclamations of the
name of YHWH. The prayer is all about YHWH, YHWH's action
and faithfulness, YHWH's uncommon generosity toward David.
The prayer is an act of celebrative praise. No fewer than eight times
does David exclaim, "Lord YHWH." The formula—consisting in
the proper name of YHWH and the solemn title "Lord"—is likely
a phrasing for God attached to the Jerusalem temple and to its
liturgy that is in turn attached to the monarchy. Thus David is
engaged in theo-political rhetoric of high style, praising God and,
at the same time, calling attention to David's own Jerusalem establishment that is derivative from God's own passion and commitment. This oft-repeated title is reinforced by the double use of
"Lord of hosts," another title for YHWH, perhaps connected to the
ark and bespeaking YHWH's military capacity as patron of the
Jerusalem establishment (vv. 26, 27). Thus the two titles together
connect both David and YHWH to the political establishment that
is willed by YHWH and presided over by David.

The connection made between the wonder of YHWH and the
realism of David is articulated in three formulations:

- You, O Lord, became their God (v. 24).
- The Lord of hosts is God over Israel (v. 26).
- For you, O Lord of hosts, the God of Israel, have made . . .
  (v. 27)

David's extravagant praise is not in a vacuum. He prays with an eye on the political domain entrusted to him. He is indeed doing "public theology" through the medium of public prayer; while he praises YHWH, the praise serves to legitimate David's domain in Israel.

The praise of YHWH that is the focus of the prayer, moreover, is accented with the "formula of incomparability" in verse 22:

> Therefore you are great, O Lord God; for there is *no one like you*, and there is no God besides you, according to all that we have heard with our ears. (2 Sam. 7:22 NRSV)

David shrewdly attaches to this formula of incomparability a second statement of incomparability, only this time asserting Israel's incomparability:

> Who is like your people, like Israel? Is there another nation on earth whose God went to redeem it as a people, and to make a name for himself, doing great and awesome things for them, by driving out before his people nations and their gods? (2 Sam. 7:23 NRSV)

The statement concerning Israel is not unlike the claim on the lips of Moses that also celebrates Israel's distinctiveness:

> For what other great nation has a god so near to it as the Lord our God is whenever we call to him? And what other great nation has statutes and ordinances as just as this entire law that I am setting before you today? (Deut. 4:7–8 NRSV)

To be sure, for both Moses and David, Israel's distinctiveness is derived from YHWH. Nonetheless, the prayer of David makes a claim for Israel's own distinctiveness, thus engaging in a bit of self-serving propaganda. The lesson is that our "public prayer" is never disconnected from political reality and never disinterested, but always in a context of acute vested interest. It is clear that David manages to keep that self-interest in check, never forgetting that it is YHWH who is the source of all the specialness enjoyed by the Davidic kingdom.

The prayer is all about praise. That praise is further emphasized when it is matched to David's deference toward YHWH. The transaction of praise is to state the enormous difference between God and the one who prays, God articulated in wonder and majesty and the one who prays as humble and insignificant. Such deference is a rhetorical means for the "magnification" of YHWH. The prayer of David begins with exactly such a gesture of deference:

> Who am I? . . . nobody!
> What's my house [dynasty]? . . . nothing!

In these words David remembers where he came from. When found by Samuel for his initial anointing, he is Jesse's eighth son, a little kid with no claim of any kind (1 Sam. 16:1–13). That he made it thus far is only due to YHWH. The transformation of the little kid into a king is a great thing for David; it is, however, a "small thing" for YHWH, a simple, effortless gesture that scarcely required any special divine effort. Thus David's posture for prayer is an acknowledgment that all that he has become and all he possesses is a pure gift of YHWH, given inexplicably in YHWH's generosity, without any claim or achievement on David's part. David acknowledges that both his life and the remarkable rise of Israel among the nations are pure gift.

The quality that makes David so remarkable in Israel is that he can remember where he came from. Unlike his arrogant son Solomon, he remains rooted in a social reality that evokes gratitude. This rootedness is evident in his narrative, from which I will cite two examples. First, in his notorious affront against Uriah and Bathsheba, when for an instant he forgot his rootedness in Israel and its Torah, he is capable of prompt and, we may be believe, genuine repentance (2 Sam. 12:13). When he is summoned by Nathan for his sin, he immediately and without argument acknowledges his affront. He has not, in his success, moved away from his covenantal rootage. Second, in a very different mode, we have the brief narrative wherein David recalls the "best drinking water" from his hometown of Bethlehem (2 Sam. 23:13–17). But he will not drink it! He will remember that the lives of his comrades are more valued than his drink of hometown water. He did not, in this narrative, think too highly of himself. The wonder of David, in the memory of Israel, is that he remains credibly as one of his fellows. He prays that way! It is in his needful dependence that he can magnify YHWH.

But having established the distance between the majesty of YHWH and his own insignificance, and having fully acknowledged his dependence on divine fidelity and generosity, David then makes a daring rhetorical move in the prayer. Three times, near the end of the prayer, David utters the adverb "and now" (vv. 25, 28, 29). This term is common in speech in the Old Testament. It signifies that everything up to this point is preliminary. Praise to YHWH is preliminary. Deference on the part of David is preliminary. "Now" we are about to get down to the real issue of the prayer; David makes a move to "close the deal" with YHWH, having established the character of the relationship.

In verse 25, the "and now" refers back to the divine oracle of verses 5–16 in which YHWH has made a promise to David which would be "forever" (vv. 13, 16), that is, for all thinkable and imaginable futures. The petition of verse 25 alludes back to that "forever" and issues to YHWH a double imperative petition: "confirm" (that is, "raise up") and "do." Do what you have promised "forever." David is now praying YHWH's oracle back to YHWH, holding YHWH to the promises and expecting YHWH to make good on those promises. For all his deference, David will not let YHWH off the hook. David will hold YHWH to YHWH's promises, perhaps in the same way a small child can remember, even after a long nap, what the parent has promised.

In verse 28, the "and now" is used a second time. Again YHWH is addressed as "Lord God" and is reminded of what YHWH has said, to do "good" for David.

In verse 29, there is a third "and now" that David's house (dynasty) may "continue forever" and be blessed forever, as YHWH has spoken. It is proper that the life-giving vitality of the monarchy should continue, always to have an heir, always to be safe and prosperous, always to flourish in the world.

We may in these three "and now" statements notice two things. First, that the term "forever" is used in verses 25 and 29; verse 28 lacks the adverb but does assert that the words of YHWH are "reliable" (true; *'emeth*). Second, all three uses appeal to what YHWH has spoken or promised, referring to the oracle of verses 6–16. In all three cases, David's prayer concludes by holding YHWH to YHWH's promises. David's prayer features doxological gratitude and a matching deferential posture. Doxology and deference, however, are only to prepare the way for David's demand that is grounded in YHWH's own utterance. David prays as an entitled king who expects to receive all that has been assured. But even before he prays as a king, he prays as an entitled Israelite, one who lives in covenant with YHWH and who relies completely on YHWH's covenantal fidelity. We are permitted to believe, at least in the short run, that the prayer to YHWH has been heard. For in 2 Samuel 8:1–14 we read a chronicle of David's military enterprises with the concluding notation, "YHWH gave victory to David wherever he went" (v. 14 NRSV). YHWH is seen and known to be keeping the oath sworn to David.

David's prayer of *doxology*, *deference*, and *demand* may be taken as a model for prayer among those who rely upon YHWH's goodness. Yet David's prayer is peculiar to him and to the divine oracle that guaranteed him. While his prayer is stylized, it is peculiarly *his prayer* concerned with *his future* from YHWH. The pattern of doxology, deference, and demand may be replicated, but at the outset we must consider the interplay of this oracle (2 Sam. 7:1–17) and this prayer (2 Sam 7:18–29) in the course of Israel's history.

There is no doubt that the promise of YHWH to David was an act of theological legitimation that functioned as well for dynastic propaganda. David's monarchy had a long run, some twenty generations through four hundred years. We may believe, moreover, that Psalm 89:12–37 represents a characteristic liturgical reiteration of the divine oracle that founded the monarchy. And we may believe that the dynasty, in temple liturgy, continued to pray the oracle back to YHWH as doxology, deference, and demand. Thus Psalm 89 reiterates the "forever" of the divine commitment:

> *Forever* I will keep my steadfast love for him,
>   and my covenant with him will stand firm.
> I will establish his line *forever*,
>   and his throne as long as the heavens endure. . . .
> but I will not remove from him my steadfast love,
>   or be false to my faithfulness.
> I will not violate my covenant,
>   or alter the word that went forth from my lips.
> Once and for all I have sworn by my holiness;
>   I will not lie to David.
> His line shall continue *forever*,
>   and his throne endure before me like the sun.
> It shall be established *forever* like the moon,
>   an enduring witness in the skies.
>   (Ps. 89:28–29, 33–37 NRSV)

The liturgy, growing out of the oracle, is utterly sure of that divine commitment.

But then the facts on the ground intruded upon the liturgical claims of royal David's city. Just after verse 37 came the Babylonian armies and the destruction of Jerusalem. Prophetic tradition asserted, moreover, that Nebuchadnezzar had been dispatched by YHWH in YHWH's rejection of the city that had failed.

If, as seems credible, the armies came against Jerusalem after Psalm 89:37 was composed, that leaves the question, What should be said in the next verse of the psalm after verse 37? The remainder of Psalm 89, verses 38–51, now speaks in a very different voice, in the cadences of loss, sadness, and abandonment. Verse 38, a different voice of prayer in Israel, makes accusation against YHWH who has reneged on the oracle to David:

> But now you have spurned and rejected him;
>   you are full of wrath against your anointed.
> You have renounced the covenant with your servant;
>   you have defiled his crown in the dust.
> You have broken through all his walls;
>   you have laid his strongholds in ruins. . . .
> You have removed the scepter from his hand,
>   and hurled his throne to the ground.
> You have cut short the days of his youth;
>   you have covered him with shame.
>   (Ps 89:38–40, 44–45 NRSV)

In verse 46 begins an aggrieved complaint that culminates with the pathos-filled wonderment of verse 49:

> Lord, where is your steadfast love of old,
>   which by your faithfulness you swore to David?
>   (Ps. 89:49 NRSV)

YHWH is addressed directly. The liturgical piece asks about YHWH's "*hesed* and faithfulness"; these are the same two words around which the Davidic monarchy had gathered from the beginning, a word pair already repeated four times in the positive part of the psalm:

> I declare that your *steadfast love* is established forever;
>   your *faithfulness* is as firm as the heavens. . . .

Righteousness and justice are the foundation of your throne;
  steadfast love and *faithfulness* go before you. . . .
My *faithfulness* and *steadfast love* shall be with him;
  and in my name his horn shall be exalted. . . .
but I will not remove from him my *steadfast love,*
  or be false to my *faithfulness.*
(Ps. 89:2, 14, 24, 33 NRSV)

The word pair attests to YHWH's passionate commitment to the monarchy and YHWH's utter reliability. And now all of that is swept away! There is no longer any sign of YHWH's fidelity to Israel, no evidence of YHWH's faithfulness to the dynasty. From of old steadfast love is the ultimate promise of the divine oracle:

But I will not take my steadfast love from him, as I took it from Saul, whom I put away from before you. (2 Sam. 7:15 NRSV)

And now it is gone! It is no wonder that in the prayer, David, in doxology, deference, and demand, had insisted that YHWH keep YHWH's promises; and now nullification!

The cadences of the promise keep ringing in Israel's ears and keep sounding in Israel's liturgy. We may believe, moreover, that the people of David kept praying the prayer of David,

- in exuberant doxology,
- in appropriate deference, and
- in uncompromising insistence.

They prayed it with such intensity that the prayer generated new oracles of promise concerning the monarchy:

The days are surely coming, says the Lord, when I will fulfill the promise I made to the house of Israel and the house of Judah. In those days and at that time I will cause a righteous Branch to spring up for David; and he shall execute justice and righteousness in the land. In those days Judah will be saved and Jerusalem will live in safety. And this is the name by which it will be called: "The Lord is our righteousness." (Jer. 33:14–16 NRSV)

They prayed it, apparently, until YHWH reiterated the old oracle and acted upon it:

Incline your ear, and come to me;
    listen, so that you may live.
I will make with you an everlasting covenant,
    my steadfast, sure love for David.
                    (Isa. 55:3 NRSV)

This promise, now spoken to forlorn exiles, reiterates the old themes:

- The covenant is eternal, not interrupted even by the crisis of Jerusalem. The old "forever" is again given divine enforcement.
- The fidelity of YHWH is asserted in the old word pair of *faithfulness* made *sure*.
- The renewed promise is rooted in David and in YHWH's commitment to David!

It turns out, in the long course of Israel's faith, that YHWH's promise persisted. Later generations could still draw on it. We are permitted to imagine that one of the reasons for divine persistence is the vigorous, demanding entitlement of David and those who prayed after him. Prayer impacts the Lord of the promise. We may even entertain the notion that without that insistent prayer uttered over and over, divine persistence might have failed.

David's prayer holds YHWH to YHWH's primal commitment. As a result, YHWH is the God who says yes to David and to Israel. There is no yes and no.

In [God] it is always "Yes." (2 Cor. 1:19 NRSV)

Without the prayer YHWH might have issued only a "perhaps." It is David's prayer that evokes YHWH's abiding fidelity. The prayer is based on the oracle, but the oracle stays alive and generative in Israel because of the prayer. The God of the oracle is praised by the people of doxological deference. But it is David's demand that pressures the God of all promises.

Questions for Reflection and Discussion

1. How can we thank God for God's grace?
2. How can our prayers remember where we came from?
3. What has God promised us, and how should we pray for it?

Chapter Five

Solomon

1 Kings 3:5–15

From the outset, Solomon was well beloved by YHWH and was destined to be king (2 Sam. 12:24–25).

But for all of that, Solomon did not receive the throne of his father David easily. The narrative of 1 Kings 1–2 reports on the problem of succession to David's throne on two counts. First, at the behest of David, Solomon proceeds to eliminate *in violent ways* his key adversaries in the struggle for the throne. In quick succession, we are told, he dispatches Adonijah, his brother; Joab, his father's lead military officer; and Shimei, a detractor who championed the continuing claim of the northern kingdom (1 Kgs. 2:13–25, 28–35, 36–46). In addition, Solomon banished the priest Abiathar from Jerusalem (vv. 26–27). Solomon's ascent to power is orchestrated in a series of killings that parallel the violent choreography of *The Godfather*.

Second, it is clear that Solomon carried out the careful plans of *intrigue* for the seizure of the throne of his father, with Nathan the prophet and his mother, Bathsheba, playing key roles in his arrival at power (1 Kgs. 1:11–37). It is clear concerning both intrigue and violence that Solomon did not come to kingship by public acclamation as had his father David. His ascent to the throne is an "insider job" that is less than noble. While the narrative is careful to exempt Solomon from direct involvement in the intrigue, it is clear that he is the key agent in the series of insider murders. Clearly, Solomon is no innocent bystander, but does what is necessary in his ruthless rise to power. He became king with no claim of innocence, for he played the games of power skillfully and intensely.

Nonetheless, Solomon's initial presentation as king is marked by innocence, the previously reported intrigue and violence notwithstanding. Perhaps that move from intrigue and violence to a new official innocence has a parallel in our own political enterprise. After a bruising political campaign marked by false representation, smear, and manipulation, the winner, now appearing in office, articulates a new public innocence as the face of governance. This new innocence may issue in a state of the union message. For Solomon, in parallel fashion, it issues in a narrative report of a royal dream. The premise of the dream is a pious, well-intended Solomon. He "loved YHWH" (1 Kgs. 3:3). He obeyed the Torah and began as an exemplar king. In his newly enacted innocence, he dreams. The report of the dream offers Solomon some distance from the rough and tumble of politics. He enters a zone of alternative reality in which he need not be in control or "on the make." He can rest back in an imagined world and count on the generous God of covenant as a real and available resource beyond any of his demanding political associates. He dreams a royal dream, imagining that his royal office is a gift from God for which he must now accept responsibility, and in which he has a choice to begin an alternative existence, an unencumbered child of the Torah.

The dream is a conversation with YHWH, a bold practice of prayer in which Solomon meets a genuine and serious "prayer partner." In the drama YHWH speaks twice; the two speeches of YHWH form an envelope that encloses Solomon's single speech. In YHWH's first speech, YHWH speaks tersely and abruptly, inviting Solomon to "ask" (v. 5). YHWH's invitation is a simple permit, not unlike that of a miraculous genie that offers three wishes. Here the divine invitation and offer are open-ended and without limit. This is the God who has loved Solomon from his

birth, ready to endow him with all that is needed for governance
(see 2 Sam. 12:24–25).

Solomon responds immediately in his single utterance in this
dream exchange (vv. 6–9). Solomon is invited to ask. But he does
not ask until verse 9. Before that he stylizes a prayer that includes
several components of prayer that we have seen in the prayer of
his father David, namely, *doxology and deference*. The opening of
his prayer is a celebration and confirmation of YHWH's abiding
fidelity to David his father. The beginning is an acknowledgment
of YHWH's *ḥesed* toward David, YHWH's fidelity that is the primary point of the oracle of 2 Sam. 7:16, a fidelity offered (vv.
28–37) and questioned (v. 49) in Psalm 89. YHWH has attended
to David and sustained him all his life long. YHWH has done so,
according to Solomon, in response to David's devotion to
YHWH, expressed here as "fidelity" (*'emeth*), righteousness
(*ṣedeqah*) and righteousness (*yashah*). Curiously, Solomon's statement would suggest that YHWH's fidelity to David is not
grounded in YHWH's commitment to David but as a response
required by David's Torah keeping that earned and expected
divine fidelity. While this curious insistence is the work of self-
conscious traditionists in Israel, it may also suggest, on Solomon's
part, that he, as David's son, has some entitlements with YHWH
as a result of David's obedience. If so, even the doxology may not
be completely innocent. In any case, David's faithfulness—
expressed in an impressive triad of traditional words—is sandwiched between two uses of the phrase "great *ḥesed*" on YHWH's
part. Thus:

- YHWH: great fidelity
- David: fidelity, righteousness, uprightness
- YHWH: great fidelity

The effect of the statement, deliberately arranged in this way, is
to bind YHWH to David and, consequently, to Solomon. Verse 6
ends with an acknowledgment that Solomon's own role as the next
king is a powerful sign of divine fidelity to David, for in the ora-

cle of 2 Samuel 7:12 YHWH had promised David a son and heir. Solomon now presents himself in that role in an acknowledgment that expresses both gratitude to YHWH and entitlement for Solomon.

The phrase "and now" in verse 7 moves the prayer beyond the memory of David to the present circumstance of Solomon. Only here in the prayer is YHWH addressed as "Lord my God," a majestic recognition of YHWH with a possessive pronoun that connects YHWH to Solomon. This part of the prayer articulates Solomon's humility, modesty, and deference to YHWH. The new king characterizes himself as only a "lad," lacking the maturity that properly belongs to kingship. More than that, Solomon confesses that he lacks competence to do the things that kings are expected to do, perhaps alluding to the king's primary responsibilities as military leader and judge. The double statement of youth and lack of competence places Solomon in a position of dependence and need, a self-characterization that situates him in readiness to receive immense divine gifts. As YHWH is generous in offering, Solomon is needful and receptive, perhaps using rhetoric to justify an immense asking that is to follow. In verse 8, the statement of dependence is followed by recognition of the demanding complexity of kingship in Israel. Solomon, according to this prayer, is ill prepared to rule and that lack of adequate preparation is rendered even more complicated by the largeness of the task. Solomon is scarcely up to it! We are able to see with Solomon, as with the prayer of his father David, that even the doxology and the deference position him for a big petition, a mix of deep need and entitlement.

Only now, in verse 9, do we arrive at the petition, which is the direct response to the divine invitation of verse 5. It is as though the prayer in verses 6–8 has helped prepare the way for the petition, creating a situation of need and dependence, so that YHWH is persuaded ahead of time to be generous. In such a setup, Solomon might have "asked for the moon," that is, made extravagant requests of this generous God. But he does not. Indeed he asks only one thing, and that one thing is not for himself. He asks only that he be equipped to be a good king; Solomon is focused on his responsibility and asks nothing for himself!

Solomon's single request is properly framed. He identifies himself as "*your* servant" and acknowledges that his task is for "*your* great people." The request is that YHWH may be properly served. Nothing of "I" or "me," only "*your* servant," "*your* great people." Finally we come to the single request. Solomon makes his petition out of his place in the triangle of YHWH-people-king. The work of the king is that the rule of YHWH should be effective among YHWH's people.

Solomon asks for a "listening heart," though the phrase in the NRSV is translated as "understanding mind." The heart, in Old Testament discernment, is the locus of decision making and can be thoughtful but also passionate. Thus Solomon asks for a well-equipped organ for decision making. The modifier "listening" perhaps suggests a twofold connection. On the one hand, he asks that the king may be attentive to the needs and petitions of the people for whom he is responsible. The word "listening" is the Hebrew term *shema'*, which draws us to the central and familiar Shema' of Deuteronomy 6:4, "Hear, O Israel." The petition is that Solomon may be attuned to the will and purpose and governance of YHWH that is attested in the Torah. The double reference to "listen" is for the sake of wise rule. The discernment of "good and evil" means to sort out what makes for life and for death, and perhaps alludes to the phrase in Genesis 2:17 wherein the human ancestors are barred from access to the mysteries held for God alone (see Deut. 29:29). Thus the request, in addition to seeking competence, may also be an embrace of covenantal tradition, the very tradition from which Solomon subsequently foolishly and destructively departs (see 1 Kgs. 11:9–10). In any case, in this prayer Solomon prepares to be a "good king."

The prayer of Solomon receives a prompt divine response (vv. 10–14), a response that exhibits the prayer as a generously dialogic transaction. First, Solomon is commended by YHWH for what he asked and for what he did not ask. He asked only for the power to discern rightly; he did not ask the things a conventional king might seek, namely, long life, wealth, and victory. Thus Solomon has exercised remarkable restraint and YHWH has responded in generosity that matches the royal restraint. YHWH gives more than is asked, when the asking is faithful and responsible. In verse 12, Solomon is endowed with a wise and discerning heart—just what he had asked. But immediately in verse 13, there is a second divine gift—"riches and honor." The double gift of *what is asked and what is not asked* anticipates the promise of Jesus to his disciples: When there is passion for God's kingdom and God's righteousness, "all these things will be yours as well" (Matt. 6:33). In Jesus' utterance, "these things" are food, drink, and clothing; in Solomon's purview they are wealth and power. But the point is the same. YHWH's generosity is well beyond human need or human asking, because YHWH wills for those who pray an abundance of well-being that can only come as God's gift. The Father-God to whom Solomon prays is not a Father who gives a stone or a snake (Matt. 7:9–10). Like any generous parent, this God is one who gives bread and fish . . . all necessary sustenance that causes life as well-being.

But in verse 14, the God who gives twice—what is asked and what is not asked—now adds a crucial condition. This verse begins with an important "if." Everything depends upon obedience to Torah so that the wonder, generosity, and abundance of prayer are kept fully within the framework of a covenantal relationship in which obedience to YHWH's will is the premise of the relationship. Thus the God to whom Israel prays (and to whom the church prays after Israel) is not a doting "sugar daddy" who responds to a wish list. The transaction of prayer modeled here is between covenantal partners who live a continuing history of mutual commitment and responsibility. The unspoken but implied negative of verse 14 is that a failure to keep Torah commandments will yield a short, unhappy life. But the accent is upon the positive. Prayer is an act situated in a lively relationship of mutuality, so that the petition is on the lips of the willingly responsive.

The transaction began as a dream (v. 5). And now the young king awakens (v. 15)! It was a dream. But "dream" does not connote fiction in the Old Testament. It refers to a moment of liminality in which the sharp distinction between God and humanity, between heaven and earth, is penetrated and human partners with God are given access to a rich face-to-face communion. In this text Israel can articulate the possibility that even the most powerful, those preoccupied with the things of this world, can and must allow occasions of dialogic vulnerability in which the petitioner pauses in the exercise of power and control to be receptive and yielding. The prayer is an act of being willing and able to ask, but able only because God has *addressed* the king and the king knows that he is *addressed*, called by God to a peculiar identity in which he remembers himself to be "your servant" and not an autonomous agent.

Such a dream moment, one that leaves Solomon vulnerable, addressed, and reassured, may come as a surprise when least expected. In Solomon's case, the dream evokes a visible, public response:

> Then Solomon awoke; it had been a dream. He came to Jerusalem where he stood before the ark of the covenant of the Lord. He offered up burnt offerings and offerings of well-being, and provided a feast for all his servants. (1 Kgs. 3:15 NRSV)

He offered up! Solomon acted with the most elemental "stuff" of life, offering "food" to YHWH in the form of a sacrifice, and food to his court circle in the form of a feast. This public act was a feast situated on YHWH's turf, and therefore gratitude and generosity are the proper order of the day.

The God with whom Solomon dreamed and to whom Solomon prayed and from whom Solomon received the gift of kingship was not yet finished with this king. In 1 Kings 9:2–9, Solomon dreams a second dream and YHWH meets him again. By this time in the narrative a great deal has happened to Solomon and to his realm. The intervening narrative would suggest that Solomon had grown jaded in office, perhaps even cynical.

Solomon seemed to be more focused on the God-given "extras" of royal office—wealth, power, and prestige—than on attending to the summons to wise rule.

Now the God who speaks is not so much generous as rigorous. In this dream, moreover, Solomon is not permitted to speak. He can only listen, as he is addressed in ways that clarify his royal responsibility. Prayer is, in this case, not words uttered to YHWH, but words spoken by YHWH to this human subject who is called to account. In this second drama that concerns Solomon in his maturity, the God of the "if" of 1 Kings 3:14 lays out uncompromising options for the king. The either/or concerns Torah obedience. If there is obedience (v. 4), there will be prosperity for the dynasty of David (v. 5). But if there is disobedience (v. 6), then there will be big trouble (vv. 7–9). Perhaps YHWH had grown weary of Solomon and was no longer patient and generous with him.

But such prayers never happen in a vacuum. We may, in a general way, trace the narrative connection between the first prayer of generosity (3:5–14) and the second prayer of a demanding either/or (9:2–9). According to the narrative, Solomon, in his long reign, had seized upon the divine extras of "riches and honor" from the first dream and had come to enjoy too much the extravagances of royal life that made his reign a spectacle on the earth (see 1 Kgs. 10:14–22, 23–25). We may judge that Solomon no longer had a "listening heart"; in his steady pursuit of wealth, power, and prestige, it is impossible to imagine that he was any longer able to "listen," either to the needs of his people or to the requirements of his God. The narrative shows that enormous extravagance makes it almost impossible to "listen." What Solomon seems to have done over his long life is to utilize his God-given wisdom, so well exhibited in the narrative of 1 Kings 3:16–28, for the foolish pursuit of conventional modes of royal sovereignty. As a consequence, the reign that started out in genuine receptivity ends up in a self-destructive absence of listening that was inherited by his son Rehoboam. He also "did not listen" (1 Kgs. 12:15). It is impossible to imagine the older Solomon or his jaded son any longer engaged in a dream transaction of vulnerability, humility, and receptivity.

Perhaps it is for this reason that Jesus, in his teaching to his disciples concerning anxiety, coveting, and faith, takes Solomon as a model for one who was not as well off as creatures who live by God's gifts:

> Consider the lilies of the field, how they grow; they neither toil nor spin, yet I tell you, even Solomon in all his glory was not clothed like one of these. (Matt. 6:28–29 NRSV; see Luke 12:27)

And Paul, in his meditation on the life and death of Jesus, considers the truth that "God's foolishness" is wiser than "human wisdom" (1 Cor. 1:25 NRSV). In the end, the *wise* Solomon turned out to be a fool, preoccupied as he was with possession of gifts that were not fully his.

This prayer of Solomon, so well probed by the instruction of Jesus and the meditation of Paul, holds together in a marvelous way *the utter generosity of God* and *the uncompromising requirements of covenantal engagement*. In Solomon's prayer the generosity of YHWH is voiced in 1 Kings 3:13:

> I give you also what you have not asked, both riches and honor all your life; no other king shall compare with you. (1 Kgs. 3:13 NRSV)

The uncompromising requirement of covenantal engagement follows in the next verse:

> If you will walk in my ways, keeping my statutes and my commandments, as your father David walked, then I will lengthen your life. (1 Kgs. 3:14 NRSV)

The two cannot be separated. If we take only the generosity of YHWH, we destroy the context for viable communion. If we take only the uncompromising requirements, we miss the readiness of God to give "abundantly far more than all we can ask or imagine" (Eph. 3:20 NRSV). Mature prayer is the capacity to enter the dream communion with God who gives and summons. Every time we awaken from such a moment, we are propelled to act from the generosity of the God that attests to the wonder of the creator and the goodness of creation.

Questions for Reflection and Discussion

1. What are the new situations and conditions for which we should pray?
2. For what kinds of wisdom should we pray?
3. How much of God's generosity should we expect?

Chapter Six

Jonah

Jonah 2:2–9

J onah's prayer in 2:2–9, set apart as the only poetry in the narrative of the book of Jonah, is the centerpiece of the book. That prayer does not occur in a vacuum, but at one moment in the ongoing vexed transaction between Jonah and his God.

Before we consider Jonah's prayer, we may review the narrative of the first chapter of Jonah, which creates a context for Jonah's prayer of thanksgiving in chapter 2. In that introductory narrative that sets the stage for the prayer, three matters are of note for our reflection:

1. Jonah is an Israelite (Hebrew) and an avowed worshiper of YHWH whom he identifies as the creator:

> "I am a Hebrew," he replied. "I worship the Lord, the God of heaven, who made the sea and the dry land." (Jonah 1:9 NRSV)

Jonah understands himself to be bound in loyalty and trust to YHWH. The confession he makes to the ship's crew accents the majestic transcendence of the God of Israel as "the God of heaven." It is, moreover, important that he credits YHWH as the one who "made the sea," for in what follows it will be crucial to the narrative that YHWH is maker and ruler of the sea.

2. Jonah is a disobedient adherent to YHWH. He is commanded by YHWH (1:2), but he flees away from the intent of YHWH (v. 3). Indeed, he attests to Israel's normative faith enough to conclude that he, in his disobedience, is the cause of "the great storm" (v. 12). Thus he fully affirms the tight calculus of Israel's faith that *disobedience* evokes divine *punishment.* These first two points—an adherent to YHWH . . . a disobedient adherent to YHWH—together articulate an irony that runs through the narrative. Jonah *knows* but does not *do* what is required, a perfect setup for a tale of divine wrath and human disaster.

3. Given Jonah's compromised faith, it is important to notice that Jonah is not the only one who prays. As the crew prepares to throw Jonah overboard and so be rid of the cause of the disaster (an action Jonah himself proposes), the crew also addresses a prayer to YHWH (v. 14). Presumably the crew is not Yahwistic or Israelite; nonetheless they accept Jonah's avowal of the God who causes the punishing storm, and so they address that same God. They are about to kill Jonah and ask that they not be judged guilty for the necessary murder. The prayer of the crew evidences great respect for the God of Israel, even if the prayer is formulaic and a conventional prayer in the midst of violence that might have called for more than conventionalism. The crew takes YHWH with more seriousness than does Jonah, even if Jonah can acknowledge his failure before YHWH.

This introductory chapter concludes with the disobedient Jonah put at risk, "into the sea" (v. 15), the sea which YHWH has created and over which YHWH presides. Consistent with Jonah's expectation and the sailors' concurrence, the expulsion of Jonah from the ship ends the storm (v. 15). The expulsion of Jonah and the cessation of the storm happen in the very same verse as a single sentence. It is as though the God of the storm wanted only to engulf Jonah, who is now profoundly at risk. Jonah, moreover, has no claim to make to YHWH and utters no petition. He is, at the end of the introductory chapter, disobedient to YHWH; his status at risk is a consequence of that disobedience. There is no hint that YHWH has done other than what is appropriate, given the faith of Israel.

The prayer of Jonah is framed in chapter 2 by two narrative notices. In verse 1, the prayer is introduced by a report that Jonah is now situated in the belly of the large fish that had been dispatched by YHWH (1:17). Indeed YHWH had "provided" the fish precisely to rescue Jonah from the threat of the sea, though that rescue itself is perhaps nothing to celebrate. For Jonah is still profoundly at risk! It is remarkable nonetheless that the fish was "ordained" by YHWH to rescue Jonah even though he had uttered no petition. More than that, he had disobeyed and had no reason to be rescued.

The prayer is followed by the narrative report that Jonah is "spewed out" from the great fish at the command of YHWH. Thus the prayer is framed by two actions of YHWH: YHWH *provided*, YHWH *commanded* the fish that did the spewing out. The second expulsion of Jonah, this time from the fish, landed Jonah on "dry land," the very "dry land" that Jonah has already confessed to belong to the realm of YHWH (1:9). Thus Jonah moves from one zone of YHWH's creation to another, from the sea to the dry land. All the while through the risk, Jonah has been in zones of creation governed by the creator God; he has never been outside the realm of YHWH's rule, for YHWH's creation comprehends both sea and land.

The prayer on the lips of Jonah is a Song of Thanksgiving, a highly stylized utterance in Israel. Notice that Jonah's prayer of thanks is spoken, in narrative sequence, while he is still in the belly of the great fish, that is, before his rescue is completed and he returns to dry land. It is likely, however, that the narrative sequence wants us to understand that the "swallowing" of Jonah by the fish is already the sign of rescue, for he is no longer "at sea," no longer subject to the whim and threat of chaotic waters. The rescue is not at this point complete, but because the fish is YHWH's instrument of rescue for him, it is not inappropriate for him to anticipate the complete rescue to dry land. Thus the fish functions in the narrative as a liminal "middle zone" between the great threat of the *sea* and the equally great safety of the *dry land*. The threat of the sea is overcome and the offer of the dry land is anticipated, and therefore thanks is an appropriate posture for an Israelite. Even though Jonah was completely recalcitrant against the will of YHWH, he was still able to pray to YHWH. It is as though the threat of the sea and the swallowing by the fish have returned him to the sanity of trust in YHWH.

This prayer, like Israel's regular practice of thanksgiving, begins with a description of the trouble from which Jonah required rescue. The simple rubric of such a prayer is, "I cried . . . you heard." But the specific lining out of this prayer is much more complex than that. The prayer begins by Jonah's memory that "I called . . . I cried" (v. 2). We have no narrative evidence of such a prayer by Jonah unless we refer to verse 1 where the verb for "pray" is much less intense than the verbs used here. Jonah cried in distress. He recognized his true situation of helplessness; he knew that he must turn to YHWH, his only means of help, and he dared to break the silence with his needy, urgent petition.

It is promptly affirmed that "You heard" (v. 2). But verse 3 does not follow easily after verse 2. If YHWH heard, then YHWH's response to the petition in verse 3 is the very antithesis of what Jonah needed. Or perhaps verse 3 looks behind verse 2 to describe how Jonah was in distress in the first place. It is clear, either way, that here the distress is credited to YHWH. That does not agree with the narrative account, in which the trouble came because the sailors, at the suggestion of Jonah, threw him into the sea. Thus Jonah misrepresents the cause of his trouble, which in fact was brought about by his own recalcitrance. Verse 3 attests to the way in which prayer can distort in self-serving ways. To credit YHWH with the distress serves to exempt Jonah himself from responsibility.

In verses 4–6a Jonah describes his situation for YHWH. In verse 4 Jonah quotes himself. He repeats his previous statement in which he acknowledges that he is remote from the temple, from the place where YHWH is present and from which YHWH's help will come. The verbal report in verse 4 is matched by Jonah's narrative account of trouble in verses 5–6a. The work of such prayer is to call YHWH's attention to trouble and need, and so to evoke divine response. Here the poetry of Jonah engages in rich hyperbole, for the actual experience of being in the sea is characterized in cosmic terms—"overwhelming waters, the deep, weeds and mountains"—as threats that robbed Jonah of freedom and a chance for survival. The language of prayer is free to employ such hyperbole; it is the sort of regressive speech that we may use in contexts of acute danger and pain. The emotive dimension of the danger is so real that it requires overstatement so that the listener can appreciate the direness of his circumstance.

Attestation to the wonder of YHWH's deliverance is limited to the simple statement of verse 6c, introduced by the preposition "yet." The "yet" is an adversative whereby the rhetoric inverts, by YHWH's saving presence, the circumstance just described. This single affirmation concerning YHWH is at the center of Jonah's prayer. For all the accent on Jonah's need, the core claim here is YHWH's power to save:

- YHWH is credited with rescue. The "You" of rescue is the same "you" who was named in verse 3 as the one who cast Jonah away. Prayer is able to credit YHWH with actions—both negative (as in v. 3) and positive (as in v. 6)—without any explanation of how this has been done.
- The rescue is to "bring up my life." The verb indicates a physical elevation, in this case lifting Jonah out of the chaotic waters. The verb is the same one Israel has used for the exodus, "to bring up out of the land of slavery." Rescue is extraction from the chaotic waters and the threat of death.
- Except here the dangerous place from which Jonah is rescued by YHWH is "the pit." Such characterizations of place are not intended to be precise. While it is "pit" here, in verse 2 it is "Sheol," whereas in the narrative it is "the sea," the embodiment of chaotic energy that negates life. Such assertive description does not aim at exactness, but at an emotive overload in order to communicate the urgency of rescue.
- The one credited with rescue is here designated as "YHWH my God." Thus YHWH is called by a proper name while the

parallel phrase "my God" indicates a history of intimate con-
nectedness. Only in this one instance in the prayer is
YHWH so fully characterized; this usage is at the center of
the prayer, while the uninflected name of YHWH is utilized
at the beginning and end of the prayer (see also v. 7):

I called *to YHWH* (v. 2).

Deliverance belongs *to YHWH* (v. 9).

Thus YHWH, at the beginning, middle, and end of the prayer,
dominates the utterance of Jonah. YHWH is the decisive player
in the dramatic transformation from trouble to restoration, from
pit to temple.

By verse 7 Jonah is finished with his attention to YHWH. Now,
in verse 7, interest is drawn back to the "I" of the speaker. In this
verse it is as though Jonah must give an account of his piety and
his readiness to turn to YHWH, a readiness that contradicts his
stance in chapter 1. Verse 7 permits Jonah to represent himself as
a pious partner of YHWH. He confesses that in his helplessness
he remembered YHWH. Evidently he did not remember
YHWH in the first chapter when he was strong and able to act in
freedom. It is as though Jonah is confessing "fox hole religion,"
turning to YHWH when he has no other source of hope. But
remembering the God whom he had forgotten is no small matter.
It is the act of remembering and so addressing YHWH that causes
his need to be noticed by the Lord of the temple.

From this assurance of being heard by the Lord of the temple,
Jonah, in verse 8, utters a propositional theological truism. The
statement does not really follow from the preceding, and reads as
though it were a quite self-conscious didactic aside, a generalization
deduced from his immediate transaction. If the verse is to be
accepted as a legitimate part of the prayer, then it means that Jonah
had come to his senses and had reengaged YHWH in an act of "loyalty." From such a vantage point he is able to reflect on the rejection of loyalty when YHWH is disregarded and devotion is given
instead to idols, that is, to unreal "vapors." Thus Jonah, congruent
with Israel's covenantal faith, articulates an unambiguous either/or.

The curiosity in the verse is that Jonah has not "worshiped" any other god, unless his own pride and willfulness against YHWH are to be understood as "vain" works of devotion. If that is the case, the verdict he renders is a quite sophisticated theological insight, to see that *willful selfishness* is indeed *false worship*. The verse does not directly indict Jonah for his previous action, but we may infer as much. Jonah has moved from willful false worship back to true loyalty, and takes his own case as a lesson for his listeners.

Now, having returned to "loyalty" in covenant, verse 9 moves to the conclusion of the prayer, an act of gratitude that consists in three gestures that are characteristic in Israel. First there are verbal thanks. Indeed the entire prayer is an act of thanks in which an Israelite gives thanks by reciting the entire drama of need and rescue. Second there is sacrifice, an offering of something of value to YHWH, acknowledging a gift from YHWH and a debt to YHWH. Third there is an acknowledgment that the thing of value offered is a fulfillment of a vow made to YHWH. It was the case that when one prayed to YHWH for deliverance, a promise was made to give a gift to YHWH when rescue had been enacted (see Ps. 116:12–19). The genuinely pious remembered the promise and fulfilled the vow. On all these counts of *verbal thanks*, offering of *sacrifice*, and fulfillment of *vow*, Jonah is here seen to be a faithful Israelite and a faithful partner to YHWH.

It is not surprising that Jonah sounds an exclamation that summarizes the outcome of the drama of rescue, and identifies the agent capable of such rescue: "Deliverance belongs to YHWH." It belongs to none other. Jonah could not save himself nor could he count on any other god. Israel has known this since the miracle of the exodus (Exod. 15:21). But every Israelite must sing the affirmation again, not only for what is remembered, but also for what is experienced directly, immediately, personally, at first hand. Jonah knows that the God of great miracles is the God who, from the temple, attends to all the needs of YHWH's people.

At the end of the prayer, having been lifted out of the sea and having dwelt three days in the liminal context of the great fish,

Jonah now is back on dry land, the threat of chaotic waters defeated (v. 10).

We have seen that this prayer is enormously complex:

- It voices in *hyperbolic fashion* deep need that must be addressed to YHWH. In Israel's prayers, full articulation of trouble in vivid imagery is a recurring practice.
- It makes visible either *deception* or *self-deception*. When Jonah accuses YHWH in verse 3 of casting him into the sea, he contradicts the "facts" of the narrative. Whether he is mistaken in this or, more likely, whether it is a deliberate rhetorical ploy against YHWH, is not clear. Either way, the accusation does not persuade, because the reader knows better.
- Along with self-deception, verse 7 suggests *self-serving piety* on the part of Jonah. He is able to report that he remembered YHWH, but does not acknowledge that he fled YHWH in an attempt to forget his mandate from YHWH. Both the self-deception and his self-serving are offered in the prayer as qualifications for a rescue to be given by YHWH.
- As often happens in such prayer, it easily slides over into *didacticism* in verse 8. Those who pray in public—and we readers are Jonah's public—do not often acknowledge that even when the prayer is addressed to God, there are other listeners. We often cannot resist the opportunity to extract from prayer theological lessons that others need to learn.
- The prayer ends in *gratitude* that we may take as genuine.

The complexity of this prayer is reflective of the complexity of all prayer. Prayer purports to be single-minded in its communication with YHWH. Everyone who prays is complex, given to deception, distortion, and willfulness; our prayers are most often thick with mixed motives, distortions, and exhibits, even if only to the self. There are "saints" who are more mature and more disciplined than this in their prayer. But evidently Jonah is not among those mature, disciplined saints. For that reason his compromising and manipulative maneuvers are highly visible in the prayer. We may spot such maneuvers in his prayer and be driven to reflect on our own acts of seduction in prayer whereby we deceive ourselves, even if God is not deceived.

Given all of that, however, the "story line" of the prayer is nonetheless clear and faithful to Israel's core faith. It is a drama of need and rescue that culminates in gratitude. None of the rhetorical byplay detracts from the clear staging of a human person in need who addresses a divine agent with generous saving power. A dramatic exchange between the two exhibits a newness in the world that could happen in no other way, a newness signified by "dry land" in verse 10, a cipher for ordered well-being after a nightmare of chaos and near death.

It is also to be noted that in verses 4 and 7 Jonah addresses YHWH in the temple. That is, even from the distance of "the sea" or within the great fish, prayer is still aimed toward Jerusalem where YHWH resides (see 1 Kgs. 8:28–30). This reiterated point makes clear that Jonah is not a private lonely individual; he prays as a member of the community that is represented in the temple liturgy. Even at a distance, he is a member of that liturgical community that receives a new world of good, safe, ordered creation from the Lord of the temple.

When Jonah ends up on "dry land," we may expect, in his gratitude, that Jonah is now ready to embrace his mission, again a dispatch by YHWH to Assyria: "Go to Nineveh" (3:1; see 1:1). Jonah goes; but before his mission is finished, he prays a second time (4:2–3). In his second prayer it is immediately clear that he has not yet come to accept his duty or the future of the world on YHWH's terms. YHWH has "turned from his anger" toward Nineveh and "changed his mind" about divine wrath against Nineveh (3:9–10). This act of divine forgiveness toward Israel's enemy evokes Jonah's anger and elicits his prayer rebuking YHWH.

In this second prayer, Jonah reiterates the old covenantal formula of Moses from Exodus 34:6–7 confirming YHWH's generous forgiveness and steadfast love. It is this hallmark of divine graciousness that galls Jonah and it is the reason he did not want to go to Nineveh. He did not want YHWH's graciousness extended to Israel's enemy. He rebukes YHWH for being who YHWH has always been in the life of Israel. Jonah wants to keep YHWH safely in his own agenda of willful parochialism; but YHWH breaks out of every such formulation. It is clear that Jonah's gratitude voiced in 2:8 has little staying power, for gratitude would have welcomed divine graciousness toward others. Like much of our well-intentioned prayer, the next exhibit of divine generosity erodes our good intent and we, like Jonah, are often back to partisan resistance. Life on YHWH's terms is beyond Jonah. He is "angry enough to die"; like Jonah we are sometimes angry enough with God to die. Sometimes, but not always.

Questions for Reflection and Discussion

1. How can we pray in the midst of our disobedience?
2. From what will God deliver and rescue us?
3. How can we pray past our own self-deception?

Chapter Seven

Jeremiah

Jeremiah 32:16–25

A s Jeremiah had long anticipated, the Babylonian army came aggressively against the city of Jerusalem and against the state of Judah. Since their first incursion into Judah in 598 BCE, the Babylonians had exercised hegemonic control over the city and the state, but this more recent assault on the city reported in Jeremiah 32:1–5 was the decisive finish of the state of Judah and its urban establishment. In short order the city was destroyed, the temple razed, the monarchy terminated, and the last king, Zedekiah, carried away into exile (2 Kgs. 25:1–17). According to prophetic discernment, moreover, this assault was not simply imperial aggression; it was an enactment of YHWH's will against recalcitrant Judah, with Nebuchadnezzar and his army simply a vehicle of divine judgment.

As things moved toward a disastrous ending for the Jerusalem establishment, prophetic faith had to find a new mode of discourse. There was, in and around Jerusalem, ample grief over the loss, a fact attested in the book of Lamentations. Such wholesale grief might have led to despair. But it did not! Rather, the prophets, most particularly Jeremiah, seized on the crisis of destruction, disaster, and displacement, and converted that venue for political *despair* into an arena of *hope*. In the specific matrix of Jerusalem, Jeremiah speaks a new word of divine possibility that is not grounded in visible circumstance but is rooted only in the conviction that the God who "plucks up and tears down" is also the God who will "plant and build" (see Jer. 31:28). Most remarkably, in the book of Jeremiah, which is permeated with invective and threat, chapters 30–33 offer a rich and sustained affirmation of new possibility that envisions the rebuilding of Jerusalem and the reconstruction of Israel as the people of YHWH.

In the midst of that extended prophetic utterance of hope, the poetry of these chapters is interrupted by the remarkable narrative of Jeremiah 32:1–15. In that narrative, Jeremiah receives a promissory word from YHWH that is dated to 587 BCE—the tenth year of King Zedekiah and the eighteenth year of Nebuchadnezzar in Babylon (32:1); the directive from YHWH is given to the prophet just at the peak of the destruction of Jerusalem. The prophet is mandated, in the midst of such social chaos, to buy the family farm in his ancestral village of Anathoth (32:7; see 1:1). This village was in the tribal territory of Benjamin, just to the north of Jerusalem, that is, right in the path of the advancing army. It is important for us to grasp the counterintuitive mandate YHWH gives to Jeremiah:

> Buy my field that is at Anathoth, for the right of redemption by purchase is yours. (Jer. 32:7 NRSV)

Jeremiah is commanded to purchase his family farm just at the moment when the military threat must have made the land nearly worthless and the prospect for productive use of the land was nil. Jeremiah is commanded to act in what must have been an uncommonly foolish way. The command of YHWH is echoed in the imperative of Jeremiah's cousin, Hanamel, in verse 8; the double mandate of verses 6 and 8 assured Jeremiah that this was a proper and required move. Because the act is "the right of redemption," Jeremiah is summoned to act as a responsible member of his family in order to keep the "inheritance" in the family. The narrative gives an account of the precise and careful way in which the land was purchased and secured through proper legal procedures (vv. 9–13).

But what interests us is the divine oracle of verses 14–15. In verse 14 the command of YHWH is to make the deeds secure so that they will persist through the crisis of social chaos. This is followed in verse 15 by a divine oracle of immense assurance:

> For thus says the Lord of hosts, the God of Israel: Houses and fields and vineyards shall again be bought in this land. (Jer. 32:15 NRSV)

After the narrative details on the transaction, this divine pronouncement which concludes the narrative report functions as verification that in time to come the land will again be productive and inhabited, and so will recover its worth. The assurance from YHWH contradicts the current facts on the ground. Land that is presently *worthless* will in time to come be *valuable*. It is none other than the God who has dispatched the army of Babylon who offers this astonishing assurance for time to come.

It is in response to this remarkable mandate and assurance from YHWH that Jeremiah speaks the prayer that is the subject of our study (vv. 16–25). The prayer is in fact an utterance of dazzled praise that celebrates the capacity of YHWH to invert the historical process as anticipated in the assurance of verse 15.

The prayer begins with a doxological acclamation in two parts. First, the prayer names YHWH "Lord God" and attributes to YHWH the wondrous capacity to be creator of heaven and earth. The language is conventional doxology that celebrates YHWH's power, language that is reminiscent of exodus rhetoric concerning "strong hand and outstretched arm" (Deut. 26:8). Second, from that declaration in verse 17, the prayer draws its conclusion:

> Nothing is impossible for you!

The emergence of creation—heaven and earth—signifies that YHWH has the power and competence to do whatever YHWH wills (see Jer. 10:12). The term "impossible" ("too hard") is likely reminiscent of the same term in Genesis 18:14 (rendered as "too wonderful") in which the promise of a son and heir to aged Sarah and Abraham is a gift from YHWH in defiance of all normal expectations. Thus the prayer begins in very large scope as a celebration of YHWH's capacity to work newness—a new heaven and earth, a new son and heir—and now a new people Israel after destruction.

From that large acclamation the prayer provides a more-or-less syllogistic assertion of the character of YHWH's governance (vv. 18–19):

Verse 18 articulates the fundamental "either/or" of this powerful God whose summons to obedience permeates all creation, and most especially the life of Israel. The prayer is a reiteration of an ancient formula from Exodus 34:6–7 that speaks of the convergence of YHWH's *gracious fidelity* and YHWH's *uncompromising sovereignty*. On the one hand, YHWH practices fidelity (*ḥesed*) in extravagant ways. On the other hand, the guilty are answerable even to the next generations. It is noteworthy that the next generations are mentioned in both the positive and negative statements, for Israel, in its moment of exilic crisis, must think about the implications of this moment for the generations yet to come. Verse 18 stresses the answerability of all to YHWH. There is no escape from the summons to covenantal obedience, which became the criterion for all that is to follow. This syllogistic formulation is followed in verses 18–19 by naming YHWH as "The Lord of hosts," that is, the military commander who is "great" and "mighty" and who keeps all of humanity under keen surveillance. YHWH's watchful monitoring is in order to operate a tight system of rewards and punishments for those who obey or disobey, for those who produce outcomes congruent with YHWH or not. The prayer remains quite generic and offers no petition. Read in context, however, the generic statement may suggest that in the sixth-century exile, in the face of dislocation, the God of all surveillance is actively assessing those who keep covenant Torah and those who do not. The impact of this assessment is to assure that nothing happens beyond the horizon of YHWH's monitoring; even the destruction of Jerusalem is in purview. The prayer does not assert that 587 is punishment, but the issue is framed so that that conclusion can be drawn. Everything is understood as an outcome of divine assessment, for good or for ill.

The middle section of the prayer, verses 20–23a, is a recital concerning YHWH's generous fidelity. The recital witnesses to Israel's most treasured miracles, and is divided into three statements, acknowledging and relishing YHWH's decisive, generous actions:

- You showed (v. 20).
- You brought (v. 21).
- You gave (v. 22).

The three statements are offered as concrete evidence that YHWH has indeed shown "steadfast love" (v. 18). Steadfast love takes the form of quite concrete historical acts:

- In the exodus YHWH established a reputation (name) as a powerful force, capable of overriding the designs of Pharaoh (v. 20). Nothing is too hard for YHWH . . . including the rescue of slaves from the oppressive forced-labor policies of Pharaoh.
- Verse 23 refers again to the exodus rescue; it alludes to YHWH's power and "outstretched arm," thus echoing the doxology of verse 17.
- The culmination of the exodus is settlement in the good land (v. 22). The prayer reiterates Israel's most elemental confession of faith, which is taken as evidence that YHWH is indeed generously faithful.

This recital of generous fidelity is abruptly broken off in verse 23 with an adversative "but" that ends the recital of divine fidelity and turns toward Israel's miserable response to such generosity. The rhetoric of verse 24 is unexpected in the midst of celebrative doxology. In this rhetoric the prophet returns to the most standard prophetic discourse of judgment and sentence, which contradicts YHWH's faithful generosity. Israel has failed completely to keep Torah. For that reason ("therefore"), all the "evil" of Babylon has come upon Israel.

The "therefore" of divine judgment as an inescapable outcome of Israel's disobedience is reinforced with the "see" ("behold") of verse 24. The city of Jerusalem is under assault by the "Babylonians" ("Chaldeans"). The assault evokes the recital of three standard curses—sword, famine, and pestilence. While the language is conventional and stylized, it is also true that war breeds famine and epidemic diseases. The conventional formulation curses are not remote from reality in the city under military assault. Since the rhetoric is a prayer addressed to YHWH, this characterization of the city can be addressed to YHWH in verse 24:

> What you spoke . . . you can see.

YHWH's word comes to actuality in visible historical modes.

The language of verses 20–24 is quite remarkable, because it places back-to-back Israel's two primal modes of theological discourse. On the one hand, as in the exposition of "steadfast love" in verse 18, verses 20–23a recite and celebrate YHWH's inexplicable and generous investment in Israel's well-being. On the other hand, as an exposition of "repay the guilty" in verse 18, verses 23b–24 exposit the rigorous "deeds-consequences" structure of covenantal faith that in prophetic discourse is presented in speeches of judgment that are organized around indictment and sentence.

Thus verses 20–23a and verses 23b–24 articulate two great themes in Old Testament faith, or better, two paradigmatic ways in which YHWH's relationship to Israel and to the world was understood and interpreted. What may challenge us is the deep tension between these two perspectives, even though they are held together in the prayer and even though the rhetoric moves easily from one to the other. We may say that verses 16–25 offer a quite self-conscious theological articulation that aims to sound key accents of faith. But we may also say that after we acknowledge such self-conscious theological intentionality, in fact our prayers, rooted in interpretive traditions, do easily and readily move back and forth between the God who freely gives and the God who appropriately punishes and rewards. We are not called on in prayer to be consistent systematic theologians, but we are able to voice everything that is important in this intense utterance of the relationship. We may imagine that the tension (or contradiction) between verses 20–23a and verses 23b–24 can be accounted for on two grounds:

- First, we are permitted to pray all the dimensions of an unresolved life and an unsettled faith. And since we are, at deep emotional as well as intellectual levels, a flood of contradictory possibilities, the tension voiced in this prayer should not surprise us. We may be variously preoccupied with YHWH's extravagant generosity or with YHWH's starchy accountability. We may, in prayer and in utterance of prayer, move quickly and without notice from the luxurious gift of generosity to a sense of our inadequacy that is called to account. The God who gives graciously may also be the God who keeps under surveillance.
- But second, such a sense would indicate not only that we may pray our unresolved tensions and our unsettled contradictions, but that the God to whom we pray is hidden, mysterious, grand and majestic, beyond all our patterns and systems of understanding. We celebrate a God of generous fidelity, but this is a God who will not be mocked. We know about a God who calls to account, but beyond accounting there is the God of immense forbearance; therefore we must voice all those traces of God's holiness without managing them too closely.

Jeremiah prays amid the wreckage and grief of Jerusalem. He knows of the tradition of fidelity and he knows that the exodus and land-giving memories are ancient impossibilities that YHWH has wrought . . . we know not how! But Jeremiah also knows, amid the wreckage, that this God is sober and on guard about obedience and disobedience. In prayer Jeremiah could not say everything at once; but he does say, through the prayer, the truths of his faith that struggle with each other.

At verse 24, Jeremiah can be sure that what YHWH says, YHWH does. It is remarkable that in the liturgical lyrics of doxology and in the prophetic speeches of judgment, the prophet manages to comment quite specifically about his time and place; and yet, even given such specificity, he offers prayer that can be prayed belatedly, even by us in our own time and place. The specificity of saving miracles and the conclusion of deep judgment read with poignant contemporaneity. That is why these same prayers to this same God still live on the lips of the faithful. By the end of verse 24, the scenario from fidelity to judgment has run its course. Generous fidelity and trenchant accountability are both possible for the God who does the impossible!

The entire prayer moves to its climactic rhetorical focus in verse 25. The concluding sentence is introduced in the NRSV with "yet," a translation that counters the judgment just voiced in verses 23b–24. In Hebrew the verse is introduced by a word usually rendered, "And now." The force of the word is to set the present moment apart from the past review that has just been concluded. The new verse, marked by "yet" or by "and now," suggests that YHWH's affirmation in verse 25 contradicts, countermands, and overcomes what has just been said. The mood is, "In spite of all of that!" The verse quotes YHWH and looks back to the divine oracle of assurance in verse 15. There YHWH had promised that the currently worthless land will again be inhabited and productive. And now, in verse 25, Jeremiah reiterates that divine assurance and indicates his own amazement at the readiness of YHWH to utter an assurance that completely contradicts present circumstance. It is overarching divine intentionality for the long run that contradicts present "facts on the ground." It is because of divine intentionality that the land is to be secured for the future, even if presently occupied by the Babylonians.

If we consider the prayer in its entirety, we can see that verse 25 with its reiteration of divine assurance looks back to verse 17 with its doxological assertion, "Nothing is too hard for you." Now we are able to see that this celebration of "divine possibility" is here not only a generic principle that is everywhere true; the statement pertains precisely to the circumstance of Jeremiah's prayer. What is not "impossible" is that YHWH will override deathly existence by an abiding resolve to do good and so to restore the land.

Jeremiah's bold prayer, a subset of Israel's bold prayer, does not accommodate or conform to present circumstance. Because of the fidelity and freedom of YHWH, who wills abundant life for Israel, Jeremiah (and Israel) can pray boldly, against present circumstance, for fresh divine resolve.

There is no doubt that this doxological affirmation of YHWH's capacity to do what the world calls impossible—and Jeremiah's capacity to trust that divine impossibility—continue to echo in the biblical tradition:

- In the divine oracle that follows the prayer of Jeremiah, YHWH picks up on Jeremiah's rhetoric and asks back to Israel, "Is anything impossible for me?" (v. 27). No direct answer is given to the question of YHWH, but the oracle makes clear that the assumed answer is no. No, nothing is impossible for YHWH. In the oracle that follows, YHWH will gather exiles (v. 37), give a new heart and a new way (v. 39), make an everlasting covenant (v. 40), and plant Israel in the land (v. 41). All of that is against the exilic facts on the ground. But YHWH can do it, such circumstance notwithstanding.
- There is no doubt that the celebration of YHWH's impossibilities, rooted in the question from Genesis 18:14 and exposited in the present prayer of Jeremiah, continues to sound in the faith of the early church in the New Testament:

  In Luke 1:37 at the beginning of the Jesus narrative, the angel, in anticipation of his birth, assures Mary that "nothing will be impossible with God."

In Mark 10:27 when Peter and the disciples see the problem of "the rich young ruler," Jesus assures them, "For
mortals it is impossible, but not for God; for God all
things are possible" (Mark 10:27).
In Jesus' prayer in Gethsemane Jesus affirms that
"For you all things are possible" (Mark 14:36).

In the end, however, the one thing not possible is that an obe-
dient Jesus should be rescued from suffering; in that suffering and
death, faith reaches the edge of God's impossibility.

• In lyrical fashion, Paul lines out the great evangelical possibilities that open the world to joy. He speaks concerning
the faith of Abraham, and declares the God of Abraham
to be the one "who gives life to the dead and calls into existence the things that do not exist" (Rom. 4:17).

In that doxological assertion Paul identifies *resurrection of the
dead* and *creation from nothing* as the signs of God's power to do the
impossible.

The church, in much of its prayer life, has been cowardly and
anemic, daring to pray only for that which the world regards as
possible. Jeremiah's prayer, so typical of Israel's bold faith, exhibits
the way in which faith hopes beyond circumstance. Faith knows
that new life—in ancient Anathoth or anywhere in the world—
arises not from what is given in the world but from the God who
makes all things new. Jeremiah is grounded in old miracles and
fully acknowledges present judgment. After all of that, however,
he says, "And now." He waits for gifts from YHWH that the
world does not expect. Such prayer is toward YHWH's future!

Questions for Reflection and Discussion

1. What impossible things is God doing now in our midst?
2. How will God hold us accountable?
3. What joy is God trying to give us?

Chapter Eight

Hezekiah

2 Kings 19:15–19

Hezekiah is reckoned as one of the two good kings in Judah after David. (The other is his great-grandson Josiah, on whom see 2 Kgs. 23:25):

> He trusted in the Lord the God of Israel; so that there was no one like him among all the kings of Judah after him, or among those who were before him. For he held fast to the Lord; he did not depart from following him but kept the commandments that the Lord commanded Moses. (2 Kgs. 18:5–6 NRSV)

As a consequence, Hezekiah was blessed by YHWH for his obedience to Torah:

> The Lord was with him; wherever he went, he prospered. He rebelled against the king of Assyria and would not serve him. (2 Kgs. 18:7)

His rebellion against the invasive hegemony of the Assyrian empire is reckoned, in biblical perspective, to be an act of trust in YHWH who is the alternative to Assyria as a source of security and well-being.

A close reading, however, indicates that Hezekiah's "true blue" trust in YHWH was not so unqualified as we have been led to believe. For we are told, a few verses later, that Hezekiah resubmitted to Assyrian authority and ceased his rebellion against Assyria as a "wrong" against the political realities of his moment. Thus the evidence on Hezekiah is somewhat mixed, as might be expected amid the ambiguous complexities of the world of imperial power where lesser powers (like Judah) had to come to terms with the empire, and yet maintain fidelity to local tradition; in the case of Hezekiah, that local tradition is trust in the God of the covenant.

Given that general context for Hezekiah's kingship in a struggle for *security* as well as *fidelity*, we focus on one particular crisis for the royal government over which Hezekiah presided. In the years 705–701 BCE, Sennacherib, then king in Assyria, continued the expansionist policies of Assyria in its effort to gain access to the Mediterranean Sea. Because Judah and its capital, Jerusalem, stood in the way of the Assyrian military intention, it is not surprising that the Assyrian army constituted a fierce and sustained threat against the city of Jerusalem and the regime of Hezekiah. The text of 2 Kings 18:17–19:37 (and in parallel, Isaiah 36:1–37:38), provides a report on the crisis of Jerusalem, the siege laid against the city, the negotiations between the Assyrians and the king, and the wonder of deliverance wrought through the work of the prophet Isaiah.

The drama of negotiation consisted in three speeches by the representative of the Assyrian Empire, the Rabshakeh, and a series of responses made by the authorities in Jerusalem. The three intimidating speeches of the empire evoke a series of surprising responses from the government in Jerusalem. Whether the confrontations are "historical" or not is disputed; either way, they are designed to characterize the crisis of faith faced by the king, a crisis of immense public proportion.

The first initiative of the mighty empire is the taunting speech of 2 Kings 18:19–25. The Assyrian ambassador asks a series of rhetorical questions that revolve around the words "confidence, rely," both terms translations of the same Hebrew word for "trust" (vv. 20–22). The Assyrian provides common-sense answers to his own questions. The question to the Jerusalem king is, "Whom do you trust?" The inference we are intended to draw, along with the king, is that Hezekiah's reference points are unreliable in the face of Assyrian power and, therefore, Hezekiah must surrender to the overriding power of Assyria. The speech proposes two nominees for Hezekiah's trust: (a) Egypt, Assyria's rival, which is portrayed as weak as a broken reed, or (b) YHWH, the God of Israel's tradition.

In verses 23–25 the Assyrian describes Judah's military vulnerability. He offers to give Jerusalem two thousand horses for battle against him if Judah can supply the two thousand soldiers to ride them. The implication is that Judah lacks the necessary soldiers, thus the humiliation of having the enemy provide weapons (horses) that he is unable to utilize. The arrogance of Assyria is based on an awareness of Judah's military deficiency, before which Assyria is able to strut in self-assurance.

To this defiant challenge, Hezekiah's advisors make only an anemic response that is an attempt at deception, an effort to conceal from the public the risk in which Jerusalem stands (v. 26). The Assyrian has been speaking Hebrew, so that all in Jerusalem could understand. The royal request is that the exchange be conducted in Aramaic, the language of international diplomacy, in order that ordinary citizens should not understand what was being said, and should not have access to the humiliation of the vulnerable king. The feeble request would be like asking an international diplomat in Washington to speak in French, the ancient European language of diplomacy, so that the negotiations could be in secret. In truth the Jerusalem response of verse 26 is no response at all, and it is readily rejected by the Assyrians (v. 27).

The second speech of challenge by the Assyrian envoy continues the embarrassment of the regime in a loud utterance of Hebrew, thus refusing the request of verse 25 (vv. 28–35). In this speech the focus is on the question of "deliverance" from the Assyrian threat, with the inevitable conclusion that there is no "deliverance" from Assyria. The twice-repeated imperative concerning YHWH, "do not," is in verses 30 and 32. Hezekiah had affirmed along with his liturgical tradition, it is suggested, that "YHWH will deliver." That, says the Assyrian, is a futile expectation. The ground for the rejection of YHWH as deliverer is a comparison of YHWH with other failed gods, the gods of Hamath and Arpad, who have been unable to resist Assyria. In imperial perspective, all the gods are the same; all of them—including YHWH—are weak and, consequently, cannot resist Assyria. From the perspective of Israel's faith, Assyria makes a theological "category mistake," because YHWH is *unlike* the other failed gods. Whether that will be true remains, in this case, to be seen.

At the center of this second Assyrian speech there is a deep threat anticipating the deportation of people from Jerusalem. The Assyrian counsels people in Jerusalem to "make peace" (surrender!) *until!* Verse 32 assures that they will be "taken away" from their homeland. The speech sounds like an assurance, but is in fact a deep threat that is consistent with Assyrian treatment of other conquered peoples, on which see the evidence of Israelite experience in 2 Kings 17:23. Thus this second speech is even more ominous than the first.

Again, the king in Jerusalem struggles to make a response to the imperial threat (vv. 36–37). The first strategy is to remain silent and ignore the threat. But that is no adequate response, because amid the fearful silence, the military threat of Assyria remains. But then the king, at the end of his resources, makes the decisive move in this narrative account. He has been surrounded by advisors who had no idea what to do in the face of the threat.

Hezekiah, pious king that he is, takes a new initiative. He dispatches his advisors to consult with the prophet Isaiah who has, until now, not been present in the narrative account of the crisis. While the cabinet officers are mediators in the royal approach to the prophet, the exchange is between king and prophet. The king's appeal to the prophet is that the prophet should "lift up your prayer" for the small community left in Jerusalem (19:4).

The prophet is recognized as the true intercessor, the one who can pray effectively on behalf of the regime. The imperative to the prophet is set in context by the message of the king. In verse 3, the king describes for the prophet the dismal circumstance of Jerusalem. The phrase "day of distress, of rebuke, of disgrace" is perhaps an anticipation of Franklin Roosevelt's well-known Pearl Harbor formula, "A day of infamy." The ground for the king's hope for prayer is "perhaps." "Perhaps" YHWH will be aware that Assyria has "mocked" YHWH. The rhetorical strategy of the king is worth notice, a strategy addressed to the prophet, and surely to YHWH beyond the prophet. The argument is not only that the king is mocked by Assyrian arrogance or that the city is humiliated by Assyria, but that YHWH as well has been belittled by Assyrian arrogance. The purpose of such prayer is to point out that YHWH's interest is also that of the king and the city.

The prophet makes response to the king (vv. 6–7). The prophetic utterance is a characteristic "salvation oracle" marked by the formula, "Do not fear." And then there is the direct divine resolve in verse 7, that "I myself" will act so that the king of Assyria will fall. Thus the second defiant speech of the empire is answered by prophetic promise. Whereas the king and his cohorts are silent (18:36), the prophet can speak. There is as of yet no divine action, only an assurance that is as credible as the reliability of the prophet.

The Assyrian delivers a third speech (19:10–13), which does not advance the argument, but reiterates themes from the first two speeches. With reference to the first speech of 18:19–25, the Assyrian again asks about "rely" and dismisses trust in YHWH as a deception (19:10). With reference to the second speech of 18:18–35, the Assyrian again poses the issue of "deliverance," and draws a conclusion by comparison (vv. 11–13). No god has delivered any nation from Assyria. No king has been kept safe by any god. Conclusion: YHWH will be as inept and inconsequential as every other god. The only option, in the purview of Assyrian theological reasoning, is that Hezekiah must surrender.

We are now prepared for Hezekiah's third response to the

Assyrian taunt. The first response was a bid for a less-public language (18:26). The second response was silence, but then a request to the prophet to pray (18:16–37; 19:2–4). Only now do we come to our proper study, the prayer of Hezekiah in response to the third challenge of Assyria. We have taken this extended path to the prayer because it is important to understand the context of acute anxiety in which the king prays. Hezekiah utters his prayer because he is completely vulnerable and has exhausted all other resources. He is a desperate king who has nowhere else to turn. In 19:2–4, the king took the trouble of following protocol to recruit Isaiah the prophet as the one who prays. By the end of the third speech, we have the impression that matters are so urgent and the king so desperate that he cannot wait for prophetic mediation. He takes his own initiative and will offer his own prayer.

The king goes to the temple in Jerusalem to pray (19:14). Perhaps there was a great royal procession wherein the king went in style to the temple. No observer, however, could fail to conclude that the king was enormously needful and vulnerable. This was a state emergency, and royal prayer in that context was a drama in response to military threat.

The prayer is highly stylized. It begins in verse 15 with a *doxology* that voices back to YHWH the identity of YHWH as the crucial ground for prayer. That doxological identity affirms that YHWH is (a) the God of Israel, committed to Israel's well-being, (b) resident in the Jerusalem temple where the cherubim sustain the throne (see 1 Kgs. 6:23–28), (c) the only God in the entire international arena, whereby the gods of Assyria are dismissed, and (d) the creator God who is responsible for and capable of the right ordering of all reality. By this doxology, so carefully delineated, the *God of all* is summoned to *the need of Israel.* YHWH, as God of all, is capable even against Assyria and its gods, but bound by covenant to act for Israel.

The doxology is followed by a *description* of the cynical brutality of Sennacherib, the Assyrian king, whom YHWH is urged to see and hear. Sennacherib is characterized as the ultimate opponent of YHWH and has set himself, in mockery, against "the living

God." The mockery consists in arrogance and autonomy, whereby Sennacherib imagines he is free in his enormous power to do what he wants without reference to the ultimate governance of YHWH. The description assumes that YHWH will be provoked by such defiance, which is a challenge to YHWH's proper claim as ruler of all. That mockery by Assyria has a theological rootage, a refusal to acknowledge YHWH. But it has practical, worldly outcomes, namely, the devastation of "nations and lands," and disrespect for the gods of those lands that are treated as disposable items. This latter point is curious, as though YHWH will be moved by Sennacherib's disrespect for other gods. Perhaps the prayer anticipates that YHWH will act in solidarity with these other disposable gods, because YHWH will rightly understand that YHWH is also on Sennacherib's list of disposable gods. The king's description portrays Sennacherib in the worst theological light as a devastator of *the earth* and mocker of *heaven*, the two realms over which YHWH, the creator, rightly presides. The description presents an autonomous king that is in defiance of the ordering of the world for which YHWH is responsible. YHWH's own sovereign majesty has been defied!

After the *doxology* and the *description* (vv. 16–18), the prayer of Hezekiah moves to its decisive *petition* in verse 19. The petition is introduced by the notable Hebrew marker, "and now," that indicates a new rhetorical maneuver on the basis of what has gone before. The "and now" appeals to the *doxology* that binds the large sovereignty of YHWH to the need of Israel, and to the *description* that portrays the Assyrian as a willful resister to the rule of YHWH. In what follows with the "and now," YHWH is identified one more time as "our" God, the God of Israel, the God to whom Israel properly turns in need (v. 15). This is followed by the dominant imperative of the entire prayer, "save us, I pray." The Assyrian had repeatedly asserted that YHWH could no more "deliver" than could the other gods. Thus the prayer is a clear refusal of the logic of the Assyrian, an insistence that YHWH is unlike the other gods, for only this God has power to deliver, even from the great power of Assyria. Thus Hezekiah voices two appeals, both to the evident need of Israel and to the singular character of YHWH who, in power to save, is not to be compared to the other gods. The king seeks an act of divine interventionist power that will be visible among the nations.

The prayer concludes with yet another motivation offered to YHWH as a reason to answer the prayer. If and when YHWH acts to save Jerusalem, all the nations will know that YHWH is the only God. The term "alone" looks back to the same term in verse 15; the double use of the word appeals to YHWH's own will to be recognized, acknowledged, worshiped, and obeyed by all nations. Thus the anticipated rescue of Jerusalem is presented as an instrument through which YHWH's sovereignty will be enhanced. This enhancement of YHWH's rule and reputation is the antithesis of the mocking of YHWH by Sennacherib that functions to diminish YHWH's rule and reputation among the nations. *Saving* Israel is also, at the same time, a means whereby YHWH may *save* face.

The prayer evokes an immediate divine response through a prophetic oracle (vv. 21–28). The prophetic utterance is parallel to the brief utterance of verses 6–7. That utterance was a response to a royal address to the prophet. Here it is a response to a royal prayer.

The divine response picks up on the theme of "mock" from verses 4 and 16 (vv. 22–23). The mocking of the Assyrian is "against the Holy One of Israel." The mocking we have witnessed is by arrogant imperial utterance. But the utterance points to imperial action that has mobilized military power, occupied the earth, and claimed mastery over forests and cities as far as the Nile River (vv. 23–24). These verses exhibit unlimited imperial ambition that is taken, in prophetic perspective, as a direct and intentional challenge to YHWH. It is YHWH alone who rules! But the empire, like all empires, usurps the rule of YHWH and claims all for self. (See the arrogance of Assyria against YHWH in Isa. 10:8–14.)

Such arrogance, however, is answered and refuted by prophetic oracle (vv. 25–28). The "I" who speaks is the voice of YHWH. It is "I" who "planned . . . determined." It is YHWH who permits Assyria to expand its military adventure and gain success. All happened within the rule of YHWH that critiques and limits imperial rule. The divine oracle turns in verse 27 with "But" . . . nothing happens in imperial conduct that is not monitored by YHWH; YHWH knows about the raging of the empire against YHWH, a chaffing at limit and accountability. And because of such imperial rage and refusal to accept that divine limit, YHWH will act against arrogance. After the imperial "I" of verses 23–24, that boasting is countered by the divine "I" of verse 28:

> I will put . . .
> I will turn you back.

The empire has reached the limit of YHWH's alliance, beyond which it cannot succeed.

After the poetic oracle of verses 21–28, the text adds two prose oracles in verses 29–31 and verses 32–34 that assure deliverance for the royal city. As a consequence, the narrative of verses 35–37 asserts that the prophetic assurances were indeed enacted. The city was saved! Hezekiah was delivered! YHWH was victorious and has trumped imperial power. The narrative of rescue is more than a little elusive, a statement that has invited much interpretive speculation. In 19:7, the divine oracle promises "a spirit" that will spread a "rumor," which scholars have interpreted as a report of a "coup" back home that placed the throne in jeopardy. In verse 35 the narrative reports "an angel" who would "strike down" imperial soldiers. Both "spirit" and "angel" suggest that this is no ordinary turn of affairs and is not subject to critical explanation. These ways of speaking are attestations in ancient Israel to the ways in which YHWH's inscrutable rule is evident in the world of international power and brutality.

The prayer of Hezekiah in 19:15–19 is quite particular in the midst of power politics. In the midst of a frightened people and in the face of overwhelming imperial power, Hezekiah nevertheless acts and speaks as a person of faith who appeals to a will and an agency that refuses conventional, worldly characterizations of power. The response to crisis is not a military mobilization by Hezekiah, but an elusiveness that attests the openness of the historical process to the impingement of YHWH beyond all conventionality. The most important promise of this text is that prayer cannot be confined to safe familial or domestic spheres of life. The most important seduction of this text is the temptation to harness "the power of prayer" to the cause of state in uncritical ways. It is surely telling that it is the lesser, vulnerable power, and not the empire, that is a faithful partner in prayer. Those of us who belong to the United States as an imperial power may take note that the transformative prayer is on the lips of those who are under threat from empire.

The text is at least an invitation to meditate upon the elusiveness of YHWH's ways in the public domain:

- an elusiveness that provided an Easter foil to the Roman authorities that executed Jesus;
- an elusiveness that evoked the fall of apartheid in South Africa with very little violence;
- an elusiveness that triggered the fall of the Soviet Union in a completely peaceable way;
- an elusiveness that continues to vex and frustrate the unprecedented, unrivaled military power of the United States.

The elusiveness is ground for possibility in a world where empires always work to foreclose possibility. God will not be mocked! It is a lesson empires always learn yet again. It is a source of hope and possibility for those who practice faith in the face of empire. It is no wonder that Isaiah's "fear not" was a source of hope, assurance, and wonderment (19:6). Empires work by fear and intimidation. The God of Israel counters such fear and intimidation by assuring presence that transforms . . . sometimes.

Questions for Reflection and Discussion

1. Where can we seek outside advice for our difficult decisions?
2. How can we pray for others?
3. How does God elude us?

Chapter Nine

Ezra

Ezra 9:6–15

Jeremiah's prayer in Jeremiah 32 is a powerful, profound rumination on the exile of the sixth century, as leading citizens in Jerusalem were deported away to Babylon. (In the seventh century, the Assyrian threat to Jerusalem promptly faded as the Assyrian empire waned. In its place, the Babylonian empire quickly appeared on the scene and in turn came against Jerusalem, in the end more effective than the Assyrians before them.) After the destruction of Jerusalem by the Babylonians and after the deportation of leading citizens to Babylon and a more general displacement of Judeans, the geopolitical history of the Ancient Near East changed decisively. That change featured the sudden demise of Babylonian power, which was displaced by the rise of Persia (contemporary Iran) under the dominating leadership of Cyrus, the first in a line of impressive and defining figures.

It is a primary claim of the Old Testament that Persia revised the harsh Babylonian policies of displacement and permitted local populations to return to their homelands. The only nonnegotiable condition of such return was that the returned populations continue to acknowledge Persian hegemony, an acknowledgment that took the form of tax payments to the Persian Empire. For the most part, the new Persian policy is regarded in the Old Testament as benign and welcome. Thus in Isaiah 45:1, Cyrus is anticipated as YHWH's messiah! And in 2 Chronicles 36:22–23, the final verse of the Hebrew Bible, anticipation of a Jewish return to Jerusalem at the behest of Cyrus the Persian is taken as the final, defining hope of Israel in the fifth century. The prayer of Ezra that we now consider is to be understood in the context of the new Persian policy of local administration under imperial hegemony.

Somewhere in the fifth century BCE (the 400s), a small, elite company of Jews returned to Jerusalem with the authority and finance of the Persian government. That return is reported in the books Ezra and Nehemiah. While there is more than a little confusion in the report, and some doubt about what in the material is historically reliable and what is ideological articulation by the community in its own interest, there is no doubt of the Persian authorization of the return. Thus reference should be made to the decree of Cyrus (Ezra 1:2–4) and to the follow-up decree of Darius (Ezra 6:2–12). While the return engineered by leading Jews is understood in the text as an act of great theological courage, it is clear that from a Persian perspective the return is a calculated imperial policy to maintain military and, therefore, taxing power without excessively provoking the local population to hostility and resistance.

The leader of the return movement, Nehemiah, is to be reckoned as a Persian appointed governor who set about to reconstitute the razed city and to restore some kind of civic order. He is presented as a wise and hard-nosed administrator who, in the face of intense local opposition, imposed a demanding order on the community. He is rigorous in the management of tax revenue, but note should also be taken of his economic response in the interest of poor Jews who were being exploited by the Jews who controlled the economy (Neh. 5:1–13).

Alongside Nehemiah, the other defining leader for the restoration of the Jewish community as a religious-political entity in Jerusalem is Ezra. While he is incidentally called a priest, he is in fact a "scribe," one who managed, interpreted, and taught from the old authoritative scrolls. In rabbinic Judaism he is regarded as the second most important figure in the tradition (after Moses), and as the founder of Judaism as a community gathered around a textual tradition. Indeed it is reckoned that the formation of a "canonical" text whereby Judaism became "The People of the Book" is connected to the defining work of Ezra. Thus Nehemiah and Ezra are to be understood as the two agents of reconstitution and restoration, Nehemiah as a civil administrator and Ezra as a bold and generative theological leader. It is important to recognize that, in the fifth century, the Jews gathered in Jerusalem had lost most of the conventional props for the maintenance of a community. The single resource that mattered the most for the reconstitution and restoration was the Torah scroll that is the beginning of the Hebrew Bible. Thus Ezra is identified as the scribe who is responsible for "the book of the law of Moses," that is, "the scroll of the Torah of Moses," the authorizing form of the tradition from which the community would ground its self-understanding and on which it would stake its future (see Neh. 8:1–8).

In current Old Testament study, Nehemiah 8 is considered a most important narrative report in which Ezra is seen to be the authoritative teacher and interpreter who will put the newly formed community of Jerusalem on sure footing. The narrative reports a dramatic meeting in Jerusalem at a city gate. The assemblage, all together inclusive of "men and women and all who could hear with understanding," gathered to hear a reading of the Torah (vv. 2–3). Ezra is the presiding officer of the meeting, but he is assisted by other leaders as well, most notably "Levites" who stand in the old tradition of covenant.

The business of the meeting was to read and hear the old sacral tradition. It is most important to note, however, that the enterprise consisted not only of reading and hearing, but of helping the listening community "understand." And for that reason the Torah was read "with interpretation" (vv. 3, 7–8). That is, the Torah was exposited, so that there is reason to think this was an early form of "textual sermon" whereby the text is explained and connected to contemporary reality. Thus the ancient text is made available as an immediate text that has defining claim on the gathered assembly. The purpose of such instruction is to help the congregation

situate itself in this particular narrative account of reality—
together with its requirements (commandments), and so to resist
other narrative accounts of reality, notably either the narrative of
heterodox Jews who did not agree with the elites from Babylon or
the Persian imperial account of reality. The intent of the meeting
is to struggle for a quite distinct identity that will have immense
ethical and sociopolitical weight for time to come. A distinct and
intentional community is formed through the process of reading,
interpreting, and hearing!

We may, in the same chapter 8, notice two consequences of this
dramatic act of interpretation. First, verses 9–12 evidence that the
hearing of the Torah (with interpretation) was a deeply moving
experience for the gathered community, as it touched deeply into
ancient identity. The community was moved to emotional
extremity. First the community "wept" at the hearing of the Torah
(v. 9). But then the leadership turned the weeping to joy (vv.
10–11), as the impact of recovered identity is a cause for joy. (On
the turn of weeping to joy, see Ps. 30:11; Luke 6:21, 25; John
16:20.) Second, in obedience to the Torah that they studied, Ezra
instituted a celebration of the Festival of Booths in which the congregation lived out-of-doors, a replication of the old sojourn
experience of risk and vulnerability (vv. 13–18). That is, the community reenacted the specific realities of the ancient memory and
thereby made that ancient memory a contemporary reality. It is of
note that the presentation of the festival is bracketed, in verses 13
and 18, by reference to Torah study. Through this bodily celebration, the present community established its identity in continuity
with the ancient community as the glad people of YHWH; it is no
wonder there was "very great rejoicing" (v. 17).

Now that we have a clear picture of the foundational work of
Ezra in generating an intentional community of obedience to
Torah, we may turn directly to Ezra 9, the subject of our study. In
the introduction to the chapter, verses 1–4, we may identify three
critical terms. First, Jews in this context understood themselves as
"holy seed," a distinct community that is marked by birth and eth-
nic continuity that is preserved for YHWH alone. The phrase is

a most particular way of voicing theological distinctiveness that is to be acted out in obedience. But second, it is acknowledged that this community has become "mixed" with non-Jews, and so violated its mandated identity (v. 2); as a result, the community is "not separated" from other peoples who do not keep the rigors of Torah. The outcome is a violation of identity and of the relation with YHWH. Third, the outcome is "faithlessness" of the community that stands vis-à-vis YHWH in a failed, pitiful condition. While this text precedes the events of Nehemiah 8, the contrast is complete. Here there is miserable failure; there the community rejoices in its recovered identity and resolve. In our prayer, Ezra prays with urgency—fasting and torn mantle—primally aware that he leads a failed community that has not maintained its identity through obedience (v. 5).

The prayer of Ezra is a masterful offer of rhetoric that we may trace in distinct and clear rhetorical maneuvers:

The prayer starts with a deep confession of sin (vv. 6–7). Ezra begins with an intimate address to God, "My God" (v. 6). In what follows, it will be "our God" (vv. 9, 10, 13) and, finally, "God of Israel" (v. 15). Here at the outset, Ezra is intimate in his confession and acknowledges his own close and abiding linkage to YHWH. But the "my" of address quickly becomes "our"—"our iniquities, our heads, our guilt, our ancestors, our iniquities, our kings, our priests." He prays on behalf of the community and moves beyond his own shame and embarrassment to that of his community. These verses, with reference to "sword, captivity, and plundering," acknowledge that the destruction of Jerusalem a century earlier was indeed justified, an outcome of systemic sin. All parts of the communal system colluded in guilt and brought devastation. No quibble here; the city got its just reward from YHWH!

The prayer turns with "and now" in verse 8. Ezra moves from meditation upon the past to contemporary reality. The present moment of restoration is "a brief moment of favor" from YHWH, indeed, an inexplicable act of grace from YHWH, inexplicable after the admission of verses 6–7. But the momentary goodness of

YHWH is only for "a remnant." Ezra is fully aware that the community has been decimated and the continuing goodness of YHWH has only a slim minority of the community as its subject. The words of Ezra seem to reflect both a deep sense of loss for "the others" and a sense of awe that for those present the chance to begin again is astonishing. Who would have thought it?!

But that moment of grace is marked by a note of realism: "We are slaves!" (v. 9) There is new life and a chance to rebuild, a chance given by YHWH's "steadfast love." That covenantal solidarity, however, is not in a vacuum. It is "before the kings of Persia." The wording would seem to be intentionally ambivalent. On the one hand, it is the Persians who fund the rebuilding; but, on the other hand, "slavery" can only refer to Persian taxation. Thus YHWH is faithful and gracious, but that fact does not cancel out the severe socioeconomic reality. Ezra is grateful to YHWH, but sober. He marvels at the moment of opportunity that YHWH has made possible, through Persia, but also voices a challenge to Persian severity.

So how to respond to this context? The prayer voices another "and now" that again draws YHWH and Ezra (and us) into an urgent moment of decision (v. 10). In verses 11–12, Ezra offers a diagnosis of the problem and proposes a proper solution. Ezra's prayer at this point is of interest because he, as in many of our prayers, cannot resist a didactic digression which he speaks directly to his contemporaries and not to YHWH. The diagnosis of the crisis is that bad conduct has made the land unbearable; the terms are "unclean, pollution, abomination," all violations of holiness and purity that are to be the hallmarks of the restored community. These negating terms look back to verses 1–2 and the acknowledgment of being "mixed" and "not separated." The preoccupation of Ezra is reflective of the general program of purity advocated by the priests who insist that Jews now must refuse to participate in a common life with non-Jews. Or more likely, the stricture is not against non-Jews but it is against Jews who are nonobservant or carelessly observant of the rules of cleanliness. It is likely that this perspective reflects the attitude of the elite Jews who returned from Babylon against the people of the land who had never been deported and who did not share the fanatical urge to obedience of the returning elites. Thus the stricture reflects conflict within the community, all of whom subscribed to YHWH.

As Ezra offers a diagnosis, so he proposes a remedy. In verse 12, with an introductory "therefore," Ezra directly addresses his contemporaries with urgent imperatives, "do not give . . . do not take . . . do not seek" "peace and prosperity" for the others. The immediate crisis is intermarriage with outsiders, likely "unclean Jews," for such uncleanness will lead again (as it already did in the past) to forfeiture of the "inheritance." Purity is the way to preserve inheritance!

The imperatives of Ezra are of interest on two counts. First, his words should be juxtaposed to the counsel of Jeremiah to the exiles in Jeremiah 29:6–7. Jeremiah had used the same language of "take . . . give" to encourage the deported to settle down, make a life, and get accustomed to dislocation. This does not mean, I assume, that Jeremiah encourages marriage to "outsiders"; it does, however, manifest an openness that is contrasted to the tone of Ezra. But more importantly, Jeremiah urged his addressees to "seek the welfare" of Babylon (Jer. 29:7). The rhetoric is exactly parallel to that of Ezra, only it is "seek" rather than "do not seek." Thus Ezra takes a position that opposes the counsel of Jeremiah, perhaps because of changed circumstance or perhaps because of a different interpretive trajectory. In any case, Ezra's urging is that the community focus on its own "cleanliness" and resist any contact that would jeopardize that purity.

Second, Ezra's didactic prayer is surely generative of the policy instituted by Nehemiah wherein foreign women were dispatched away from Israel, because such wives, with their own religious commitments, jeopardized the community of purity (Neh. 13:23–31; see 13:1–3). The absolute claims of Torah and the dread recognition of guilt have converged to lead to this didactic urgency right in the middle of the prayer.

In verse 13 Ezra has finished his digression focusing on conduct

(vv. 11–12). Now he returns to address YHWH again. Ezra addresses YHWH and poses two rhetorical questions. The first question has a long premise in verse 13 that reiterates previous points about the legitimacy of punishment and the wonder of the remnant. The question posed in verse 14 concerns disobedience through intermarriage, a point that looks back to verses 1–4. The question requires a vigorous response of "No!" "No" because that violation of commandment would be an abomination. The second question in verse 14 pertains to the consequence of such a dread act: "Yes!" "Yes," YHWH would be intensely angry and would end the project of Israel, even the surviving remnant. The rhetorical questions are, ostensibly, addressed directly to YHWH. It is clear, nevertheless, that the questions are in fact addressed to the congregation and are offered as a way of reinforcing the imperatives of verse 12. Thus we see that all of verses 10–14, even though stated in the form of a prayer, constitute a sermonic response to the prayer that offers diagnosis, instruction, and warning. The sum of the parts is to evoke zealous obedience in the tradition of purity, for it is impurity that has caused the remembered crisis upon which Ezra dwells.

Finally, the prayer reaches its climax in verse 15. Again there is direct address, this time to "YHWH, God of Israel." The core affirmation is that "you are just." The term rendered "just" characterizes YHWH as one who is equitable, fair, reliable, and even generous. It is possible as well to take the adjective in an active way, that YHWH is the one who acts to "rectify." This statement is surely made in response to any suspicion that YHWH is unjust or unfair, or that YHWH's negating actions against Israel are unwarranted or unjustified. Such a thought must have occurred to Israel as it pondered its suffering, a thought articulated in the long poem of Job, which may have been circulating at the time. There may have been wonderment about the faithfulness of YHWH. In this utterance, Ezra, reliable teacher that he is, nullifies the question. It is not clear how the following sentence relates to that declaration, but it seems probable that the affirmation of remnant is offered as confirming evidence that YHWH is "just." It is

YHWH's gracious justice that makes the Ezra community even possible. If YHWH were less than "just," there would be no remnant . . . and no Ezra. Thus the sequence of phrases interprets YHWH's "justice" as mercy.

The last sentence of the prayer is remarkable. Its terms seem clear enough, even if its intent is a bit unclear. After the review of guilt, slavery, and remnant, and after the imperatives to purity, Ezra positions the community before YHWH "without one plea." Finally Judah, in its failure as a community of purity and as a remnant with new possibility, must present itself undefended before YHWH. Ezra knows and Judah knows that the reality of guilt continues to be defining for the community. But it presents itself in the hope (conviction?) that, in the end, it is not guilt that will shape this meeting with YHWH. Judah is unworthy and unqualified. That is clear enough. But Judah has nowhere else to turn. It turns in needy dependence to the God it has scandalized. In its lack of qualification, Judah can only say, "Here we are!" Here we are in guilt! Here we are in need! Here we are in uncleanness! Here we are in slavery! But here we are! The phrase moves beyond all the defining impediments that are so unmistakable in the text. We are *before you* whom we cannot *face*. In Hebrew the two terms "before" and "face" are the same. We "face" the one whom we cannot "face," and count on "steadfast love" (v. 9) and "favor" (v. 8) and "justice" (v. 15). There is no alternative, and Ezra would not seek one.

The prayer in fact divides into two parts, together with the whimsical plea of verse 15. The first part of the prayer is a confession, which ends with an affirmation of "new life" as YHWH's gift (vv. 6–9). This section turns on the "yet" of verse 9 that affirms that YHWH has not abandoned them. The second half of the prayer in verses 10–14 concerns urgent obedience to the command of purity. It is easy to read that concern for "purity" as punctilious moralism, as Christians have often done. We must recognize that the community is in a struggle for its very existence and is convinced that attentiveness to a *distinct identity* is urgent. Thus we can see that while the prayer deals with the constants of "sin and grace," the prayer is of interest in two other regards.

First, it is clearly linked to specific context. Ezra's prayer is uttered in a concrete crisis. Second, the prayer is not really petition, for it does not ask anything of God. The prayer functions to evoke a resolved response for determined obedience. Thus the tilt of the prayer toward didacticism does not surprise us. The community that prays must live out the urgency of its true situation before God. The concluding "here we are" counts on YHWH's presence with and for them. But it asks nothing. The recognition of that "here we are" leads to a resolve to put faith to concrete and disciplined practice. The prayer thus is congruent with rejoicing in Ezra's Torah instruction and with the crisis of the community that is threatened with loss of identity. The prayer functions to recall the community to its singular identity, unmixed and uncompromised, committed to the one who is the source of identity and the only possible giver of "new life" in the future.

Questions for Reflection and Discussion

1. What sins do we need to confess in our prayer?
2. How can we pray for a new start and a second chance?
3. What kind of distinct identity can form the basis for our prayer?

Chapter Ten

Nehemiah

Nehemiah 1:4–11

Nehemiah, a civic leader and political force, lives in the world of Ezra that is sketched out in the preceding discussion. He also is a Jew living under Persian rule, having established himself as an important official in the Persian imperial regime with access to the emperor. He is a competent, trusted servant of the empire, but he is a Jew whose heart and passion continue to be rooted in Jerusalem. He is a descendant of those deported from Jerusalem by the Babylonians; his family has well survived the transition from Babylonian to Persian hegemony, all the while with an abiding Jewish passion.

The prayer of Nehemiah that begins the book of Nehemiah, as well as the political mission of Nehemiah to Jerusalem, is introduced by a narrative report in 1:1–3. There are complex and unresolved historical questions about the Nehemiah materials, but we may give our attention to the text as it stands. A whole new episode in the interface between displaced Jews and the empire is triggered by a report brought to Nehemiah in the Persian capital, Susa, by one of his own brothers, Hanani. It is evident that there must have been reasonably easy exchange between the capital and the colony, between Susa and Jerusalem.

The report brought to Nehemiah is a shocker for him, as he learns about the status of the city of Jerusalem a very long time after the Babylonian destruction of the city in 587 BCE. The report is divided into two parts. First, he gets a report on the "survivors" in Jerusalem, the ones who remained there and were not deported by the Babylonians. It is most likely that all of the important and influential people had been deported by the Babylonians. Those who remained in the city were of less importance and influence. Nonetheless they were still there and had to cope with all of the devastation of the war that had destroyed the infrastructure of the city. It is remarkable that the report focuses on the "survivors," because the elite Jews who had been deported were condescending toward them and pretty much disregarded their existence. Nonetheless their "trouble and shame" is a measure of the destitute circumstance of the city, a measure that will move Nehemiah to action.

Second, the report brought to Nehemiah's awareness not only the "survivors" but the physical condition of the city, specifically the wall and the gates. Obviously the city lacked the most rudimentary security system and the "survivors" were in jeopardy. Beyond that, the continued devastation of the city—after 150 years!—indicated neglect and lack of responsiveness . . . and perhaps suggested to Nehemiah that the city was no adequate place for YHWH's presence. To this "urban planner," the physical, social, and theological dimensions of the report all converge to present a circumstance of dismay and dejection.

It is not surprising that the report evokes grief in Nehemiah, passionate Jerusalem-loving force that he was. Indeed, Nehemiah is representative of the elite Jews in the Diaspora who had not given up their Jerusalem-based Jewish identity, for whom the well-being of Jerusalem was an abiding agenda. Nehemiah's response to the report, that he "sat down and wept," indicates that this shrewd, competent public figure was reduced to unrestrained dismay. The word pair "sat down and wept" is the same phrase that occurs in Psalm 137:1 concerning the grief of the deportees; likely the narrative derives the phrase from the psalm, for the two acts of sadness pertain to the entire community that cares about the forlorn city. Nehemiah strikes a posture of penitence, deeply based in a theological assumption that the abiding devastation of the city is divine punishment for the sin of Israel.

The prayer begins with an address that seeks God's attentive presence (vv. 5–6a). YHWH is addressed as "God of heaven," an appellation for YHWH that bespeaks YHWH's transcendent majesty and likely reflects the conventional rhetoric of the Persian context. The God of heaven is "great and fearful." The language alludes to the power and majesty of the creator God who governs all. Yet in predictable Jewish fashion, this awesome creator God is the one who "keeps steadfast covenantal love" with Torah-keepers, that is, with Israel. (See the same connection of creation and covenant with Israel in Jer. 10:16; Ps. 147:19–20.) The double phrase positions Nehemiah before YHWH with an accent on *divine power* of a cosmic kind and *divine fidelity* of an Israelite kind. In such rhetoric, Nehemiah exhibits the cadences already voiced in the older tradition of Deuteronomy:

> Although heaven and the heaven of heavens belong to the Lord your God, the earth with all that is in it, yet the Lord set his heart in love on your ancestors alone and chose you, their descendants after them, out of all the peoples, as it is today. (Deut. 10:14–15 NRSV)

It is at the core of Israel's faith that *the creator God* with unlimited power—even over Persia—is *the covenant God* committed to Israel. That is the ground of petition to which YHWH is urged to attend.

Nehemiah's address to YHWH, after the initial bid for an audience, is a confession of "sin," a statement that matches the mourning and fasting of verse 4 (vv. 6b–7). Nehemiah's interpretation of the fate of Jerusalem is firmly fixed in Deuteronomic assumptions of a Torah pattern of obedience-prosperity, disobedience-adversity (Deut. 30:15–20). There is no thought that the destroyers of Jerusalem were ferocious and out of control. Nor is there any thought that YHWH may have been fickle or negligent. In other places in Old Testament texts, both of these responses are voiced, blaming either the oppressor nation or YHWH. But not here! Here it is all Israelite "sin," the term used three times in verse 6, a term exposited in verse 7 by specific reference to the "commandments of Moses" and by the double use of the term rendered "offend deeply," or in other rendering, "acted corruptly." The confession of Nehemiah, on behalf of his family and his people, acknowledges fault and affirms that YHWH's destruction of Jerusalem was fully justified.

The prayer turns abruptly in verse 8 with a petition to YHWH that YHWH should remember YHWH's previous resolve to be a God of forgiveness. The words of verses 8–9, introduced by petition, reflect tight syllogistic theology that situates YHWH in a two-stage pattern of *judgment and restoration*, a pattern that became decisive for Israel as "into exile" and "out of exile." That two-stage articulation of YHWH's intention is faithful to Israel's lived experience, but it is also deeply rooted in the imagination of Israel. In Jeremiah 31:28, YHWH proclaims two "watchings" of judgment and restoration:

> And just as I have watched over them to pluck up and break down, to overthrow, destroy, and bring evil, so I will watch over them to build and to plant, says the Lord. (Jer. 31:28 NRSV)

And in Jeremiah 31:10, the same two moves are voiced, though with one different term:

> Hear the word of the Lord, O nations,
>   and declare it in the coastlands far away;
> say, "He who *scattered* Israel will *gather* him,
>   and will keep him as a shepherd a flock." (NRSV)

Nehemiah's statement purports to quote YHWH's word to Moses, but the statement only roughly reflects YHWH's previous commitment. In Deuteronomy 30:1–5, YHWH asserts a promise of restoration based on divine compassion that will lead to a "gathering," but that statement assumes a previous "scattering."

In both cases and in exilic theology generally, the accent is on the "gathering," the homecoming of Diaspora Jews; in that tradition the divine promise depends upon the new resolve of Israel to obey Torah. Thus Nehemiah's petition and reminder to YHWH of YHWH's resolve is situated in a deep tradition of hope that affirms that exile, dislocation, and displacement are not the end of the story of God with Israel. There is to be a new chapter in that story that is rooted in divine resolve. The prayer of Nehemiah functions to remind YHWH of this divine resolve and to urge its present enactment to counter the unbearable condition of "scattering" that is reflected in the shambles of razed Jerusalem. Out of a memory of divine commitment, the prayer summons YHWH to enact a future that is only possible if YHWH acts yet again. In verses 6–7, Nehemiah has already lined out the "return" required in verse 9 as a precondition of newness; he does so through an act of confession of sin and new resolve.

After the "quote" of YHWH in verses 8–9, Nehemiah adds an additional statement that functions as motivation to YHWH (v. 10). Nehemiah reminds YHWH that "they," the Jews now scattered, exposed, and vulnerable, are "your servants" and "your people." That is, YHWH has responsibility for them, because from the outset YHWH has been their progenitor, advocate, and patron. This motif echoes the outrage of Moses in Numbers 11:11–12, wherein Moses reminds YHWH that Israel is YHWH's responsibility and not that of Moses. So here the community of Israel continues to be YHWH's responsibility. The ground for that is the exodus from Egypt. The verb "redeem" is supported by the standard phrases of exodus language, "great power and strong hand." YHWH acted to emancipate Israel and has since that moment taken Israel as a special charge and a special object of attention and practice. Thus two key terms of verse 9, "gather, bring," are sandwiched between the two claims upon YHWH. Before that verse, there is the appeal to the old divine promise (v. 8). After that verse, there is appeal to the act of exodus (v. 10). Both the promise and the marvelous deliverance have placed YHWH under obligation to act to create new futures for Israel. It is remarkable that Nehemiah, for all his confession of guilt earlier in the prayer, can nonetheless stand before YHWH and make insistent demand of YHWH by appealing to YHWH's past actions. Nehemiah bids YHWH to act in congruity with what Israel has known and seen in the past of YHWH. Nehemiah's sense of guilt for himself and for his family and for his people does nothing to diminish the boldness of his claim on YHWH. This unblinking appeal prepares the way for the specific petitions that follow in verse 11.

In verse 11, Nehemiah now names YHWH a second time, the first time since the beginning of the prayer in verse 5. We now have much "content" for the divine name Nehemiah utters. YHWH is

- the great, awesome God;
- the one who keeps covenant and steadfast love;
- the one who promises to gather;
- the one with great power and strong hand;
- the one who has redeemed Israel.

When Nehemiah begins in verse 11 with the name "YHWH," all of that conviction of faith is present in the transaction. YHWH is addressed and summoned. The name is introduced in verse 11 with a Hebrew particle (*'ana'*), which regularly introduces imperative petitions with a sense of urgency.

All of the prayer has been building to this moment of appeal. It is a prayer that YHWH should heed (ears attentive) the petition that is offered by Nehemiah and his community. Like all of Israel, Nehemiah does not doubt YHWH's power and YHWH's capacity to deliver. The crucial problem in Israel's prayer is getting YHWH's attention and moving YHWH to act in YHWH's great power. The reason YHWH may be expected to heed the petition is that Nehemiah and the ones who pray with him delight to honor YHWH's name, to fear YHWH's name, to take YHWH's name with utter seriousness. They are the ones who obey the commands and who enhance YHWH over all rival gods. Like much of Israel's prayer, Nehemiah assumes that YHWH is eager for magnification, is aware of the competition of other gods, and is pleased to be enhanced by praise and obedience. The petition of Nehemiah does not go so far as bargaining; unlike some psalmists, Nehemiah never threatens to withhold praise and obedience, so that the prayer is not a *quid pro quo*. But Nehemiah does indeed point out to YHWH that the transaction is of mutual benefit to both parties. YHWH also gains from a faithful transaction, namely, the enhancement of reputation.

The first part of verse 11 is a setup and preparation for what follows in the verse. Now Nehemiah utters the big imperative petition toward which the prayer has moved. The verb of petition is causative, "cause to prosper." The imperative is followed by an emphatic particle often rendered "I pray thee," and the recipient of such a gift from YHWH is "your servant." Nehemiah had already identified himself in that way earlier in the verse. Thus Nehemiah positions himself in a lowly posture of subservience. The verb "prosper" itself is of special interest because of its indeterminate quality. The verse does not name something in particular that YHWH may do. It is the verb used to describe the finding of a good wife for Isaac (Gen. 24:21, 40), and to describe the rise of Joseph in the court of Pharaoh (Gen. 39:3, 23). It refers to pragmatic worldly success. In these uses, however, it is affirmed that YHWH is effectively engaged in such worldly issues, though of course the workings of YHWH are hidden and inexplicable.

The verb "give success" ("cause to prosper") is parallel in Nehemiah's statement to "give to him mercies." This again is a remarkable petition, for the rhetoric makes a connection between the divine giver of "mercy" and the worldly reality of "that man." Except for the imagination of faith exhibited in this prayer, one would not think to connect "mercy" and empire." But that is the way of daring prayer. Because everything in the prayer is uttered under the aegis of the creator God, matters are connected and interfaced and intertwined in ways that can never be apart from the rule of God. "That man" refers in the prayer to the king of

Persia, the current leader of the great superpower. Behind this petition lies a great deal of reflection on the connection of mercy and empire:

- In Jeremiah 42:11–12 the rhetoric assures that YHWH will show mercy and the Babylonian king will consequently be merciful to the Jews:

  > Do not be afraid of the king of Babylon, as you have been; do not be afraid of him, says the Lord, for I am with you, to save you and to rescue you from his hand. I will grant you mercy, and he will have mercy on you and restore you to your native soil. (Jer. 42:11–12 NRSV)

  It is clear that the Babylonian king is subordinate to YHWH and is expected to replicate YHWH's mercy, thereby assuring that the public process of governance will be marked by compassion.
- In Isaiah 47:6, the king of Babylon is rebuked for not showing mercy, for mercy is the nonnegotiable expectation of YHWH.
- In Daniel 4:27, moreover, the destabilized king of Babylon is addressed by Daniel, the wise Jew. The king is urged by the Jew to practice mercy, even though such a posture would have been completely alien to the empire.

These texts, together with the prayer of Nehemiah, make an enormous assumption about the public world of power, namely, that YHWH's will, purpose, and governance are definingly pertinent to the practice of power in the world. Thus Nehemiah directly and simply links faith and power, so that YHWH's gift of mercy can impinge upon public policy.

The strange convergence of success and mercy means that Nehemiah seeks a gain of a concrete kind in the visible, pragmatic world of public policy and practice. But such "success" is not likely in the normal workings of empire. It will require an initiative of divine mercy in order that public processes can be reshaped according to the needs of Jerusalem.

We may linger over the divine target of "that man." The reference is not identified, but Nehemiah who prays, YHWH who is addressed in the prayer, and we readers, know who it is. We need only peek at the second chapter of Nehemiah to see that it is Artaxerxes, the great emperor of the Persian realm, whose reach of power was nearly to the ends of the earth. Nehemiah is a practical man. He becomes the urban planner who directs the rebuilding of ruined Jerusalem, for which he needs authorization and resources. He knows from the outset that the emperor is the only source of authorization or finance, and his aim is to secure that backing . . . which he subsequently does. Indeed, in Nehemiah 2:1–8, he receives that which he most needs and for which he prays.

The worldly capacity of Nehemiah, this man of prayer, is everywhere evident in the narrative. At the end of the prayer in verse 11, we learn that he is a "cupbearer," that is, a highly placed imperial official with ready access to the emperor. If his title indicated direction of the royal table, he was in a position to have poisoned the king; thus he enjoys the trust and confidence of the king. The narrative of 2:1–8, moreover, evidences that Nehemiah is shrewd in his conduct before the king. He is appropriately deferential and knows exactly when to say what. But he is also exactingly intentional, so that at the proper moment he knows what he wants and does not hesitate to ask. Twice he asks, each time with the deferential preface, "If it pleases the king" (2:5, 7). Twice he receives what he asks: (a) permission to go to Jerusalem (2:5), and (b) authorization to secure the necessary materials for rebuilding (vv. 7–8). The negotiation he conducts plays upon Jewish need, personal sadness, and the generous policy of Persia that supported local context. That would be enough to explain the transaction at the king's table. But the pragmatist is also a man of piety. For that reason, at the conclusion of the parley, he affirms that the good outcome is a gift of God:

> And the king granted me what I asked, for the gracious hand of my God was upon me. (Neh. 2:8 NRSV)

That is, his prayer is answered. Later on, when Nehemiah meets resistance from the local population, his answer to Sanballat, Tobiah, and Geshem again appeals to his religious passion:

> Then I replied to them, "The God of heaven is the one who will give us success, and we his servants are going to start building; but you have no share or claim or historic right in Jerusalem." (Neh. 2:20)

It is "the God of heaven" to whom he has prayed (see 1:5). The term "success" ("prosper") is the same one he used in prayer in 1:11. Thus with both the Persian king and with his detractors, Nehemiah's prayer is the taproot of his energy. On all counts he is vindicated.

We may in particular see in juxtaposition Nehemiah's address to God (1:5–11) and his address to Artaxerxes (2:5–8). In both cases Nehemiah's speech and conduct are powerfully intentional. He knows the outcome he seeks. In his prayer, the voicing of doxology (1:5), petition (1:6a), and confession (1:6b–8) all move to the petition of verse 11. In his address to the king, his deference plus his show of sadness serve the double request of verses 5–7. In both cases Nehemiah is capable of a careful rhetorical strategy in order to move ahead with his intentional plan. His speech to the king is in response to the king's query, "What do you request?" (2:4).

Remarkably, between the king's query and Nehemiah's response, there is a pause in the narrative:

> So I prayed. (2:4)

The prayer at this dramatic moment surely is an echo of the petition of 1:11, an echo that is acknowledged as effective in verse 8. It was the "graciousness" (*tov*) of the God of heaven that turned imperial policy toward his mission and toward the holy city that awaited restoration. The prayer is in the midst of public issues. God, in this articulation, does not "do" anything! Except that everything depends on the hidden effectiveness of God, who moves the transaction to "success."

Because of divine resolve, Nehemiah and his movement prospered in Jerusalem. That prosperity depends on Persian generosity that Nehemiah exploits to the full. But we should not miss the counternotion that is subsequently sounded in the text concerning Persia, a counternotion that is voiced in the second great prayer of Ezra in Nehemiah 9:6–37. In this prayer, a parallel to Ezra's prayer that we have considered in Ezra 9, Ezra again reviews the failed history of Israel in the presence of YHWH, a "gracious and merciful God" (Neh. 9:31). In Nehemiah 9:33, Ezra asserts to YHWH, as he did in Ezra 9:25, "You are just." That is the fallback gospel of the Jews. When all else fails, YHWH is still a reliable source of well-being. From that premise Ezra then moves to a lament that implies a petition. He describes for God the exploited status of the Jews in Jerusalem at the hands of the Persians:

> Here we are, slaves to this day—slaves in the land that you gave to our ancestors to enjoy its fruit and its good gifts. Its rich yield goes to the kings whom you have set over us because of our sins; they have power also over our bodies and over our livestock at their pleasure, and we are in great distress. (Neh. 9:36–37)

For all of the generosity and support of Artaxerxes for Nehemiah, the Persians are effective tax collectors. They exploit the colony of Yehud so vigorously that Ezra can say, "We are slaves." (Yehud is the new name for Judean territory as a province of the Persian empire.) The Jews are back at work in the homeland, but are exploited peasants. The produce and wealth generated by their labor is siphoned off by "the kings whom you have set over us," that is, the Persians. The Persians, like the ancient Egyptians remembered in Israel, have "power over our bodies and our livestock" (see Gen. 47:17–19).

The end of it all is, "We are in great distress" (Neh. 9:37).

Nehemiah's moment of success (given by the God of heaven) did not alter the requirements of imperial economics. And so Yehud must pray to YHWH again, always in a complaint, always in hope, always with petition (here implied). For all the palpable reality of the political economy, the Jews must turn again in prayer. For they are weak and vulnerable. They have no other source of appeal. The final appeal is to the God who is "gracious and merciful" in all dealings (9:31). Ezra, like Nehemiah, knows *the facts on the ground*. These, however, are submitted to *the God of heaven*. Ezra and Nehemiah and those who join their prayer trust that the will of the God of heaven will be visibly enacted in the earth. The life of the world depends, so they confess, on the "great mercies" of God, mercies that may evoke mercy even in an empire. (See Neh. 1:11, wherein divine mercy may eventuate in imperial mercy.) So they hoped! And so they prayed!

Questions for Reflection and Discussion

1. How do we pray in the midst of our grief and loss?
2. How does God call us to new "gatherings" now?
3. When do we need to pause in order to pray?

Chapter Eleven

Daniel

Daniel 9:3–19

The prayer of Daniel is given a narrative introduction in verses 1–2, and receives a divine response in verses 20–27.

The narrative introduction in verses 1–2 is of interest on two counts. First, the mention of Darius, together with his pedigree, purports to locate Daniel in the midst of the Persian Empire, for Darius was an early and great king of Persia in the sixth century BCE. It is a common interpretive judgment, however, that this dating functions as a disguise for the actual situation of the text of Daniel in the second century BCE. In that later context, Judaism was under assault from the Syrians, who attempted to wipe out the distinctiveness of Jewishness. It is not necessary for us to adjudicate between the traditional historical locus in the *sixth century* and the critically judged locus of the text in the *second century*. It is sufficient to see that the figure of Daniel is situated in an imperial context, when the hegemonic power is typically hostile to a distinctive local identity and practice, in this case the distinctive local identity and practice of Judaism.

Second, the phrasing of "the books of the number of years" connects the text to the tradition of Jeremiah, and indicates that the text is situated in a religious milieu of numerical calculations that assumes that the will of God is rigidly laid out in stages and periods, and that these stages and periods, though they are secret, may be known by special sages. The reference to Jeremiah appears to be to Jeremiah 25:11–12, 29:10, wherein the earlier prophet declares that the exile and dislocation are to be for seventy years. Before the number was frozen into a rigid system of calculation, in Jeremiah's case it was likely that the number was not to be taken with too much precision. The number seventy serves two functions, to assert that the deportation was real and would last a while, and to assert that the deportation would be limited and come to an end. Jews were not fated to dislocation to perpetuity.

Thus it is in the context of *imperial reality* (whether Persian or Hellenistic) and in the environment of *prophetic realism and hope* that Daniel prays. The narrative introduction reports that Daniel prayed a confession in an act of penitence in order to seek an answer. The text does not articulate the question to which Daniel seeks an answer, but given *imperial reality* and *prophetic hope*, both of which are reinforced in the narrative introduction, the question of Daniel (and of Jews more generally) must have been, "What is the future for the Jews?" The question in the second century was an acute one, given the harsh cultural attack on Jewish faith and practice. In such circumstance, it does not surprise us that Daniel, the model Jew, turns to YHWH in prayer, for surely a future for the people of Daniel can only be given by YHWH. Daniel and his ilk expect no future from the empire!

In that context, Daniel's prayer is one of confession (vv. 3–4a). Verses 4–14 are a stringent, unrelenting admission of guilt on the part of Israel, fully and without reservation acknowledging that the destruction of Jerusalem was deserved as divine punishment; for that reason there is no question about the rightness of God's vigorous judgment. Clearly the prayer is situated in the tight covenantal calculus of the tradition of Deuteronomy, perhaps mediated through the memory of Jeremiah, that violation of Torah commands certainly and inescapably will lead to an enactment of covenant curses. Daniel accepts the punishment as just and fully accepts that defining theological assumption that connects guilt and punishment.

The particular articulation of guilt, sin, and failure evokes, on

Daniel's part, a rich flow of rhetoric. Thus in verses 5–7, we have: "sinned . . . done wrong . . . acted wickedly . . . rebelled . . . turned aside . . . not listened." Daniel offers no excuse or mitigating circumstance, only a direct, simple acknowledgment. The norm for this indictment is both "Torah" and "prophets." The entire instructional tradition has been violated!

The consequence of such blatant disregard is "open shame," that is, visible, public humiliation (vv. 7–10). The confession of guilt is reiterated: "treachery . . . sin . . . rebellion . . . not listen." These verses repeat the foregoing confession, but here Daniel alludes to the consequences for such action, namely, that Jews are made to suffer in ways that all nations can see. The "shame" is the embarrassment for a distinctive practice in the face of hegemony that has not worked successfully. Jews have trusted in this particular God and championed a particular practice (Torah) that claimed a moral coherence (see Deut. 4:7–8), all of which is now exposed as dysfunctional. The shame is broad and deep enough to touch all Jews. It concerns those "near," the ones who remained in Jerusalem and were never deported; it impacts those "far away," the ones deported to alien lands, most particularly to Babylon, from whence comes the emergence of hope-filled Judaism. Being Jewish has now become a scandal in the eyes of other peoples. The shame concerns Israel but, as we shall see, it also brings humiliation on YHWH, for it is YHWH's people and YHWH's city that are now exhibited as consummate failures.

The confession of sin continues in verses 11–14; the violation of Torah, the refusal to listen, and the practice of sin are confirmed by heavy rhetoric that reinforces the already voiced admission of guilt. The acknowledgment of punishment is framed in verses 11 and 14 by reference to the verb *shema‘* (hear, obey) that is used negatively. That confession would seem to be a direct reference to the core imperative of Deuteronomy 6:4. Inside that frame, the prayer twice mentions "the Torah of Moses " (vv. 11, 13), and alludes to the covenant curses in verse 11 with reference to the long recital of covenant curses in Deuteronomy 28. Alongside *violation of Torah* is the refusal of "his words," likely reference to *prophetic oracles*, so that Israel rejects "the law and the prophets." Daniel's prayer thus is to be understood against the foundational covenantal requirements of Deuteronomy.

As portrayed here, Israel is completely recalcitrant. Not only did Israel refuse to hear and obey; beyond that blatant disobedience, Israel did not "turn" (v. 13). That word is thick with meaning for Jeremiah and means to reverse course and re-embrace the Torah (see Jer. 4:1–2). Behind Jeremiah is the tradition of Deuteronomy that anticipates that the exiles will turn (Deut. 30:1–10), and the derivative verdict that Israel rejected the prophetic imperative of "turn":

> Yet the Lord warned Israel and Judah by every prophet and every seer, saying, *"Turn* from your evil ways and keep my commandments and my statutes, in accordance with all the law that I commanded your ancestors and that I sent to you by my servants the prophets." They would not listen but were stubborn, as their ancestors had been, who did not believe in the Lord their God. (2 Kgs. 17:13–14 NRSV)

The prayer of Daniel, moreover, anticipates that the expected "turn" entails not only Torah obedience (which it does), but also re-embracing YHWH's fidelity. The chance that Israel had rejected was not only *obedience to Torah* but the opportunity for *a relationship of fidelity*. In its autonomy Israel had rejected both command and covenant. The inescapable divine response to such resistance was YHWH's decisive act (v. 14). Daniel's rhetoric is an echo of Jeremiah 31:28 with the same term "watch." YHWH, the offended covenant party, destined Israel to "calamity." YHWH, moreover, is fully in the right (*saddiq*, on which see Ezra 9:15, Neh. 9:33). The covenant calculus has worked reliably. YHWH is justified in the punishing destruction; Israel's recalcitrance has brought merited dislocation.

If Daniel's prayer had ended there, it would not be very interesting or compelling. It would yield nothing more than one more quite familiar articulation of Israel's old covenant symmetry, which is known to us in Psalm 1, the beginning point of all of Israel's covenantal reflection:

> for the Lord watches over the way of the righteous,
>   but the way of the wicked will perish.
>
> (Ps. 1:6 NRSV)

We should not fail to note that already in Daniel 9:4–14, the voicing of sustained confession of sin is interlaced with a counter-conviction to which appeal will be made in the latter part of the prayer:

- In verse 4, at the outset of the prayer, the God to whom Daniel prays is not only powerful ("great and awesome") but also one who "keeps covenant and steadfast love." To be sure, the assertion of divine fidelity is qualified by the recognition that it applies only to the covenant faithful. Nevertheless, the dynamism of divine fidelity is in purview from the beginning of the prayer.
- In verse 9, the ante of hope in positive divine inclination is upped. In that verse, YHWH is of course marked by covenant fidelity; beyond that, Daniel knows this is the God of *compassion and forgiveness.* Unlike the terms in verse 4, here there is no condition of obedience; these attributes belong to YHWH without reservation.
- In verse 13, the prayer acknowledges YHWH's fidelity (*'emeth*), YHWH's reliable commitment to Israel.

When one considers the cluster of terms from verses 4, 9, and 13, the cumulative effect is stunning. YHWH is the reliable, generous one, to be even more fully appreciated as a contrast to Israel, here described as unreliable in every regard. Fortunately the prayer does not end with the "full stop" of disobedience and calamity in verse 14. It is a rhetorical and theological wonder that the prayer continues beyond verse 14; it is the second part of the prayer, beginning in verse 15, that moves toward an alternative.

In these later verses, Daniel appeals to the characterization of YHWH offered in verses 4, 9, and 13, and thereby dares to continue the prayer, even after the decisive acknowledgments of disqualifying sin we have considered.

In verse 15, as we have seen so often elsewhere, the prayer moves to contemporary appeal with "and now" (*w'attah*). Given all of the past failure of Israel just recited, the wonder of Daniel's prayer (and of Israel's prayer more generally) is that Israel can continue to pray. Now, in verses 15–16, YHWH is addressed in doxology that recalls YHWH's primal deliverance of Israel from Egypt and celebrates YHWH's reputation (name) as a deliverer. The doxology in verse 15 is prelude to the petition of verse 16: "turn" away from your anger and wrath, according to your "righteousness" that is exhibited in generosity. What a mouthful! The prayer plays with the word "turn." It concedes that Israel did not "turn" (v. 13) and now asks YHWH to "turn" as Israel did not. The double use of "turn" calls to mind the double use of the same term in Psalm 90, albeit to somewhat different effect. In the psalm, YHWH summons Israel to turn:

> You *turn* us back to dust,
>   and say, "*Turn* back, you mortals."
>   (Ps. 90:3 NRSV)

But then Israel asks YHWH to "turn" and enact compassion and steadfast love:

> *Turn*, O Lord! How long?
>   Have compassion on your servants!
> Satisfy us in the morning with your steadfast love,
>   so that we may rejoice and be glad all our days.
>   (Ps. 90:13–14)

Israel knows that YHWH is able and perhaps willing to turn, as Israel is not. Thus the prayer of Daniel asks YHWH to relinquish the very anger against Israel in which YHWH is fully justified. This is clearly an appeal to the God who can forgive (as in Dan. 9:9).

In verse 17 the prayer moves to a second "and now" (*w'attah*) that further intensifies present-tense petition. In verses 17–19 the prayer abounds in imperatives addressed to YHWH. This is remarkable in light of the heavy accent on Israel's guilt, for one might judge that Israel has forfeited its right to petition YHWH. But of course that is exactly the point of the many imperatives; Israel, completely disqualified, still addresses YHWH.

The petitions are thick with tradition:

- "listen" (as Israel has refused to do) (v. 17);
- "let your face shine" (v. 17).

The phrase reflects the old priestly conviction that YHWH's presence in the temple is as a bright light, a shining face. This is a familiar formula in the classic benediction, "The Lord cause his face to shine upon you" (Num. 6:25). Israel (in the words of Daniel), amid divine *absence*, prays for *presence*:

- "incline your ear . . . hear" (v. 18);
- "open your eyes . . . look" (v. 18);
- "forgive" (v. 19);
- "listen" (v. 19);
- "act" (v. 19);
- "do not delay" (v. 10).

The urgency of petition is grounded in the dangerous, sorry situation of the faithful . . . whether in the sixth century or in the second century. Either way, the holy city is in need. If YHWH will notice, YHWH will surely act in restorative ways.

Israel has no ground for such an urgent appeal, no right to ask anything of YHWH. This is fully acknowledged in verse 18, which contrasts Israel's failed "righteousness" and YHWH's "many mercies." Again the rhetoric seems to echo Deuteronomy, where it is affirmed that YHWH chose Israel, but "not because of my righteousness" (Deut. 9:5). The possibility of forgiveness and reconciliation and the granting of a new future rest completely in YHWH's generous inclination upon which Israel throws itself in need. This language of *disqualification* and *divine graciousness* is at the core of the prayer. It will be familiar to Christians who regularly confess sin and do "not presume to come" into God's presence, who affirm that they approach the divine presence "without one plea." It was an obvious move in the church's tradition to transpose this drama of "sin and forgiveness" into christological categories; but it is important to recognize that the terms of this dramatic transaction are already fully set and voiced in the neediness and passionate conviction of Israel. The God to whom Daniel prayed on behalf of Israel is a God of profound mercy, capable of reaching out in compassion to a disqualified people. This divine capacity is the ground of Israel's future!

In these latter verses of urgent petition, one can detect Daniel's anxiety about YHWH's readiness to forgive. And so Daniel, in characteristic Israelite fashion, offers to YHWH motivation for such a generous act that has been asked. Verses 15–19 are formed by reference to the divine name (reputation):

- your name renowned (v. 15)
- your people bear your name (v. 19)

The status and destiny of Israel and of Jerusalem reflect on YHWH's reputation. For that reason Daniel proposes to YHWH that the divine act of forgiveness is "for your own sake" (vv. 17, 19), so that the world can see what a wonder YHWH is. Israel's future depends upon YHWH's self-regard! It is an enormous act of daring to pray in this way after such a profound acknowledgment of guilt. Daniel can do so because he is convinced, as is all Israel, that YHWH's future is deeply linked to Israel's future.

This is the same daring conviction out of which Ezekiel can imagine a future for Israel. That future is not out of Israel's merit or, according to Ezekiel, even out of divine love for Israel. It is, rather, out of *divine self-regard*:

Therefore say to the house of Israel, Thus says the Lord
God: It is not for your sake, O house of Israel, that I am about
to act, but for the sake of my holy name, which you have pro-
faned among the nations to which you came. . . . It is not for
your sake that I will act, says the Lord God; let that be known
to you. Be ashamed and dismayed for your ways, O house of
Israel. (Ezek. 36:22, 32 NRSV)

Thus the prayer proposes that for Israel to have a future, YHWH
must be willing to relinquish the past that is such an affront to
YHWH.

Daniel prayed in daring faith, but of course he did not know of
the divine response he would receive, because YHWH is not an
automaton. YHWH is a free agent, and so Israel prays always in
hope. But Daniel is glad to report that he received from YHWH
an immediate response (Dan. 9:20–27). In both verses 20 and 21,
the narrator uses the same adverb "while," that is, instantaneously.
Such rhetoric indicates that YHWH did not need to ponder or
calculate about Daniel's petition. The divine answer is prompt and
pertinent (vv. 20–21).

While the prayer of Daniel is cast in quite conventional
Deuteronomic language, the response of verses 22–27 reminds us
that the book of Daniel is situated in and reflects a belated and
quite distinct context in developing Judaism. In that environment,
often marked by the term "apocalyptic," we begin to hear of
"angels" (messengers) who bring the divine word and offer calculations that become ever more precise and chronological.

In this case the divine response to Daniel's prayer is through
"the man" Gabriel who appears to Daniel in a vision. First, in
verses 22–23, the messenger Gabriel reflects on Daniel who is to
receive, for Israel, the divine answer. In that apocalyptic context
messages are delivered only to the mediators who are peculiarly
qualified to receive and understand the messages that will determine the future. Daniel is to be endowed with "wisdom and
understanding," so that he can fully discern the divine decree for
the future. Beyond that, Daniel is "greatly beloved." The term

ḥmd is the word used in other places as "covet"; that is, Daniel is much desired and praised by the God who has heard his prayer. These verses serve to certify Daniel as a proper voice who can receive and interpret God's intent for the future.

Second, the actual divine message is deeply coded in numerical language that we need not here decode, if indeed we were able to do so (vv. 24–27). While the prayer has been introduced by reference to Jeremiah's "seventy years," now the divine response speaks variously of "seventy weeks" and seven weeks and sixty-two weeks. Two things seem clear in this oracular utterance. First, this is a lament concerning the suffering that Israel must endure. The punishment is not open-ended but will run its course according to divine intent. Second, during that time and within its limits, the punishment is real and the suffering is acute.

While the "time line" is obscure, it is clear that in its main outline, the prayer and response remain faithful to the primary motifs in the tradition of Jeremiah:

> And just as I have watched over them to pluck up and break down, to overthrow, destroy, and bring evil, so I will watch over them to build and to plant, says the Lord. (Jer. 31:28 NRSV)

YHWH is a "watcher" (see Dan 9:14). The seventy years or seventy weeks constitute a time for "plucking up and tearing down," but there is a limit to that. The good news from Gabriel, also by way of Jeremiah, is that there will come a time to "restore and build," a phrasing congruent with Jeremiah's "plant and build" (v. 25). The entire drama of Israel's life with YHWH consists in *suffering and restoration*. The suffering is linked to disobedience, but that is not the final word.

It is remarkable that though this chapter began with reference to *Darius*, the Persian emperor is completely forgotten by the end of *Gabriel's* pronouncement. As the chapter develops, the narrator clearly has no interest in the empire or in the time line of the empire. The chapter assumes and articulates a very different narrative in which the empire is absent and irrelevant. Israel's life is on God's time. That time is marked by "seventy," but the "seventy" culminates in forgiveness and beginning again. The Jews, in the time of Daniel, had for good reason concluded that human agency is of "little help" (Dan. 11:34). But the assurance of Gabriel is that the "help" of YHWH is more than adequate for the crisis faced.

The prayer of Daniel is a prayer of the faithful *in extremis*. It is rooted in Israel's core tradition of covenant, based in Deuteronomy and transmitted by Jeremiah. And while the absolutes of faith are here drawn into the odd categories of contemporary apocalyptic discourse, the constancies of covenant still prevail. Those constancies suggest that sin is real and Israel must come before YHWH in its failure. That reality, however, is overwhelmed by the more elemental assurance of divine fidelity and forgiveness. Guilt by itself is no adequate stance for prayer. The faithful know and always pray not from "our righteousness," but on the basis of "your great mercies" (v. 18). It is that divine mercy that assures an end to suffering and the beginning again for which Israel hopes.

Questions for Reflection and Discussion

1. How can we pray when we feel lost or dislocated?
2. What are the worldly and imperial powers about which we need to pray?
3. How can we call God to faithfulness?

Chapter Twelve

Job

Job 42:1–6

J ob, as an artfully crafted figure, is a representative of Israel's faith as it is exhibited in daring, irreverent, subversive prayer. No doubt it can be debated whether Job's utterances can count as prayer, for some of his speech is simply angered rumination not noticeably addressed to God. It is not for nothing that his name means "adversary," for Job is in an urgent contestation with all parties—with God, with his friends, with his own moral code that he has trusted for so long, and with the abusive, violent way in which the world is ordered. Thus we may give Job our attention precisely because he refuses all the pious conventionalities and will speak from the core of his hurt and from his deep, unrestrained sense of not being taken seriously. His was indeed a cry from the heart. It happens, eventually, that his cry was heard by God. More than that, he receives an answer from God that by any conventional measure is no answer at all, for the God of the whirlwind refuses to be drawn into Job's demanding calculations.

Before approaching Job's final utterance, we may consider two representative passages in his adversarial utterance against God. Job faces a profound theological contradiction, because his experience of suffering does not square with the explanatory calculus of his pious friends, a calculus to which he himself remains committed. The drama of the book of Job unfolds as Job struggles with a conventional piety that fosters submission to God in full confidence of God's reliable equity. Two of Job's most adversarial, demanding utterances indicate his deep vacillation about that calculus and about the extent to which he will trust, before God, the raw, palpable reality of his own experience of suffering.

On the one hand, in 9:19–24, Job is *ready to throw over the entire calculus* of justice because he is convinced, in his own misery, that God is unjust and unreliable, and does not perform by fair standards:

> Though I am innocent, my own mouth would condemn me;
>> though I am blameless, he would prove me perverse.
>>>   (Job 9:20 NRSV)

Job accuses God of convicting (and punishing) him though he is blameless. Here Job demands—and does not receive—the acquittal that is his due. Consequently, he rejects the entire system of God's justice.

On the other hand, in Job 31:35–37, his last utterance before God's appearance in the poem, Job assumes an almost Promethean posture and is prepared to offer a self-defense in court. Here he will still conduct himself *within the usual system of reward and punishment*, and he has no doubt he can gain acquittal. The problem is that he cannot get a court date or hearing, because God refuses to participate in the adjudication that the conventional moral calculus requires:

> Oh, that I had one to hear me!
> (Here is my signature! let the Almighty answer me!)
> Oh, that I had the indictment written by my adversary!
>   (Job 31:35)

These two shrill assertions go in opposite directions. The first, in chapter 9, proposes to overthrow the system; the second, in chapter 31, continues in the system, but demands that the system should function. Both aggressive statements, in very different ways, mount an enormous challenge to God who is presented by

Job's friends as an equitable judge who governs the world in reliable ways, who metes out prosperity and adversity according to just claims. Job's experience tells him otherwise, and the old, tired orthodoxy championed here offers no answer for him.

And so Job must wait! He must wait a very long time, because God does not speak or appear, or even take notice of Job's need or his demand. The rhetorical strategy of the book of Job is to keep God absent and unresponsive as long as possible, in the interest of heightened dramatic tension.

Finally, after a wait through eons of suffering, God speaks (38:1). But the God who speaks does not engage Job's pain or Job's challenge. God exhibits no empathy toward Job or any need to respond to Job's frontal challenge against God's unconvincing ways of working. God refuses to participate in Job's challenge and effectively changes the subject, displaying complete indifference to Job's bodily anguish and to Job's moral perplexity. The God who speaks is a God of wondrous grandeur, magnificent power, sublime beauty, and remoteness from human travail. This is not a God to whom to turn in need, even though Job has indeed turned precisely to this God in need. The God whom Job expected, to whom he prayed and offered challenge, is not the God who addresses him in the whirlwind. This God comes as a completely disorienting surprise to him.

God speaks a lyrical doxology of self-congratulation, celebrating the splendor of creation, the awesomeness of specific creatures, and the wondrous reality that the mysteries of creation are well beyond human comprehension or explanation. That is, God moves quickly past Job's litigious confrontation as if Job had not spoken, as if Job's moral quibbles are of no interest at all to the Almighty.

Only once in this long divine utterance is God's speech interrupted to permit Job to answer. In 40:1–2, YHWH invites Job to join issue, but the invitation is issued in a tone of divine defiance. God calls Job a "litigator" ("faultfinder") and adjudicator ("arguer"), terms that are dismissive, because such litigation stands no chance in the face of the awesome creator God.

Job's response to God's defiant invitation is deferential, a refusal to engage (40:3–5). It is as though Job now recognizes the wonder and power and splendor of YHWH, and thereby becomes aware of his own inadequacy for such an exchange. Job in fact refuses the divine invitation and falls back in silence, a silence that is immediately occupied by aggressive divine utterance (Job 40:6). The speech of God continues through 41:34, an ode to the wonder of Behemoth (40:15–24) and of Leviathan (41:1–34). In God's characterization of Behemoth, God speaks admiringly, and then asserts to Job, "Behemoth, which I made just as I made you" (40:15 NSRV). It is as though God—in praise of boldness, fierceness, and assertive freedom—recognizes that Job is like the most majestic of the creatures, intended by the creator to exercise boldness, fierceness, and freedom. By the end of chapter 41, the boastful creator God is finished. No more can be said! There is a pause, a silence; perhaps the poet wondered along with the reader what could possibly be said by anyone after such a glorious celebration of creatureliness!

Finally we come to Job's prayer (42:1–6). In 40:3–5, Job had in fact not answered the creator God. Perhaps Job was not yet ready to respond, or perhaps his response is withheld until now for strategic reasons. In any case, Job now answers the divine rhetorical avalanche in a way he did not in his first opportunity in 40:3–5. Job's utterance may be reckoned as a prayer because it is addressed to God. It is curious, however, because in this case, unlike most other examples of prayer we have considered, it is a *response* to a word from God. The engagement has been anticipated by Job's sustained complaint. But in fact the engagement has been initiated by YHWH's self-regarding statement. And now Job must find a way to engage the celebrative self-regard of YHWH that has removed Job's complaint from consideration. Job's long utterance of grievance has been declared by God to be irrelevant and off the table.

Job speaks a second time and is ready now to answer (42:1–6). His prayer consists in three statements that are organized around two quotations from YHWH:

- Job's statement (v. 2)
- quote from God (v. 3a; see 38:2)
- Job's statement (v. 3b)
- quote from God (v. 4; see 38:2)
- Job's statement (vv. 5–6)

1. Job's initial response is a doxology that acknowledges the wonder, splendor, and power of YHWH (v. 2). Job has arrived at that certitude about YHWH. Job does not doubt YHWH's capacity to do whatever God intends. This in fact represents no real advance in Job's theological thought. Job has never doubted God's limitless power, a power he has already acknowledged in doxology (9:5–12). Job had already asked, "Who will say to him, 'What are you doing?'"(Job 9:12). And he knows the correct answer to his question: No one! No one can question God, not even Job. He knows that, but he questions anyway. Now he reinforces his settled conviction: God is beyond limitation, explanation, accountability.

2. Job quotes God from 38:2 (v. 3). The quote is not precise, but close enough to see that Job intends it as a quote. The quote from God's lips is dismissive of questioners who prattle without competence, who thereby only obscure what everyone should know. Job quotes the dismissive statement and means that he himself has been a "hider," a "darkener" of what is known. He admits that he has gone beyond his competence in violating the boundary between God and creatureliness that is a "no go zone."

3. As a consequence of that question with its implied answer, "Who? . . . me!" Job draws a conclusion: "Therefore" (v. 3b). He now concedes that his probe of the hiddenness of God was inappropriate and he did not know what he was doing. The most important term in this acknowledgment is "wonderful," a term that bespeaks God's awesome transcendence that cannot be contained in any conventional explanation. Job recognizes that his attempt to wrap the awesomeness of YHWH in his categories was a bad effort.

4. In verse 4, Job again quotes God from the beginning of

YHWH's utterance (38:3). The first part of the statement is defiant, but the second part is a correct quote: "I ask . . . you give answer." There is no doubt who is conducting the interview. Job has assumed the role of questioner. But that is not his proper role. In YHWH's long celebrative speech, it is the creator who asks all the questions:

- Where were you . . . ? (38:4)
- Have you commanded . . . ? (38:12)
- Have you entered . . . ? (38:16)
- Have you entered . . . ? (38:22)
- Can you bind the chains . . . ? (38:31)
- Can you hunt the prey . . . ? (38:39)
- Do you know . . . ? (39:1)
- Do you give the horse its might? (39:19)

The questions go on and on. YHWH does not pause to let Job answer, because the answers are obvious. The questions are designed to re-situate Job in his posture of prayer as a creature who must submit to the creator. Job has been daring and excessively assertive, but such a stance will not work with the God of the whirlwind!

5. Job's final utterance, in 42:5–6, is in two parts. First, Job concedes that he has learned what he did not know. What he had *heard*—by conventional instruction—he now *sees*—by direct confrontation. He is now postured very differently. Second, he draws a conclusion with a "therefore" that is parallel to the "therefore" of verse 3. But Job's "final answer" in verse 6 is not as straightforward as we might take it to be at first glance, and so we must linger over it.

We are accustomed to a conventional pious rendering of the verse, the kind reflected in the NRSV:

> Therefore I despise myself,
>   and repent in dust and ashes.
>   (Job 42:6)

In this rendering, Job seems to concede everything to YHWH on YHWH's terms, and to retract his rigorous challenge to YHWH. And that may be what is intended by the verse.

If we are to take Job's prayer seriously, however, we may pay attention to recent critical scholarship that suggests that Job's final statement is much more enigmatic than our usual translations suggest. In fact every term in the final statement is problematic and may by design keep issues open and unsettled, without clear resolution:

- The phrase "despise myself" in fact lacks the object "myself" and may mean that Job rejects his small thinking and limited scope about creation.
- The word rendered "repent" in conventional church usage is related to guilt and confession, but in fact the term means, "to change one's mind." And the preposition translated "in" is better rendered "concerning," that is, "change my mind concerning dust and ashes.
- The phrase "dust and ashes" about which Job changes his mind may mean that he refuses the self-abnegation to which he has been pressed by his friends.

When we take all of these problematic terms together and try to make coherent sense out of them, the outcome may permit us to understand Job afresh as God's creature who is not destined by God for groveling submissiveness, even to God. Rather, in God's image, Job considers himself to be not unlike the Behemoth of 40:15, willed by God for boldness, fierceness, and freedom, anything but docile submissiveness. The verse may be one of self-assertion that defies God's dismissiveness.

This way of reading 42:6 contradicts our usual translations and our conventional pieties. But it is the tilt of current critical interpretation. At the very least we are put on notice that we need not thoughtlessly accept a conventional reading of the verse just because it is conventional. If, however, we are to focus on the task of prayer instead the task of exegesis, then the fact that 42:6 is ambiguous—and perhaps intentionally so—may be a clue to mature prayer. Simple, direct, childlike prayer has a certain kind of innocence to it, and we are accustomed to such cadences in prayer. But mature prayer that has passed through the unresolve of deep suffering may not settle for the obvious. It may be that there is an important place in prayer for a kind of playfulness and gamesmanship, in which the one who prays thrusts and parries and gives God no simple partnership and no obvious target for condescension. It may be that the author of the book of Job teases the reader and requires us to decide about the prayer. Or inside the text itself, it may be that Job will finally leave God guessing: Is Job pious? Did Job submit? Is Job in defiance? Perhaps the ambiguity of the prayer is not unlike that which might be displayed by a clever person before an authority figure, at the edge of *chutzpah* that is cloaked carefully in a kind of deniability, so that one is not easily convicted of affront.

If this is a correct interpretation of the difficult verse—as current critical interpretation might suggest—the prayer is an act of an adult with an adult God. This person is not easily submissive, not directly defiant, but acts in part covertly so as not to be exposed to the raw power of holiness. Such prayer may leave unanswered the opening question of Satan to God: "Does Job fear God for nothing?" (1:9 NRSV). The question and the book of Job recognize that even in our own prayer, we are not single-minded and simple in relation to God. At the very bottom, faith is a mix of *glad submissive trust* and *defiant self-respect* that will not easily yield, even in the face of holiness. Job has said too much, lived too long, and suffered too deeply to yield himself to a God who is powerful but less than trustworthy. What Job knows is that he must appear before God. He must give answer for himself. But he must take care that after he answers, there is still "a self" that has not been abandoned. Thus 42:6 may be an exhibit of a *self before God* that offers an address to God that makes possible a genuine sense of self.

When Job finished his prayer in 42:6, the book of Job might have ended in this enigmatic way. But of course the book of Job continues beyond Job's prayer with eleven verses of prose closure. The two final paragraphs we may take as divine response to Job's prayer.

In 42:7–9 YHWH has yet one more exchange with Job, a most surprising reprise. God gives a verdict on the *words of the friends and on the words of Job*. The friends are convicted and condemned for their false speech; the verdict suggests God's rejection of pious conventions that force suffering into orthodox explanations. By contrast, Job's words are "correct." The verdict given by YHWH is enigmatic, for it is not clear what words of Job are in purview. If it is correct that 42:6 is an act of defiance and a refusal to capitulate, then 42:6 is congruent with Job's extended protest. It is, I suggest, this powerful practice of *dissent from explanatory orthodoxy* as challenge to God's rectitude that is approved by God. If this is so, then the paragraph sanctions prayer that is vigorous, defiant, self-assertive, and daring enough to approach God "like a prince" (31:37), without groveling deference. On this reading God prefers a "prayer partner" who is like Behemoth . . . strong, ferocious, and free in daring ways.

Given such approval, Job has other prayers yet to pray. He must pray for his friends, for those who tried to restrain and reprimand and silence him. In the end, moreover, we are told that Job's prayer for the friends is "accepted." Job has, by his daring courage before God, earned the capacity as an effective intercessor, as an effective litigator in God's court, a petitioner who can move God from wrath to mercy. Job knew all along, it turns out, that one must not cater to the arbitrary wrath of God, but must expose it for what it is. It turns out that Job's long rhetorical enterprise has functioned to summon God out beyond God's wrath. In his prayer, Job imagined and hoped for a world better than the one God has heretofore inhabited.

In the final paragraph of the book, Job receives from God a restoration of all that has been lost in his season of suffering (42:10–17). Surely that is what Job had most hoped for. When he refused "dust and ashes," he positioned himself as an entitled creature of God prepared to secure again all that suffering had denied him. He receives a full restoration! Except that we are sobered on one point. Job receives in this final act of divine generosity—along with sheep, camels, oxen, and donkeys—seven new sons and three new, beautiful daughters.

The narrative leaves it at that. The narrative does not call attention to one other fact, but perhaps hopes we will notice. In this lavish restoration, what Job does not—emphatically *not*—receive back are the seven sons and three daughters that he lost at the beginning of the narrative "in a great wind" (Job 1:2, 19). He got everything new . . . but not what he had lost that he most treasured.

Anyone who has had a son or a daughter—and has lost a son or a daughter—knows that no new son or daughter will ever fill the void of loss. God answers prayer! Yes! God accepts the prayer of Job! Yes! But answered prayer cannot, in this instance, override or nullify loss. Even with prayer answered, Job must live his life with a huge abyss of grief at its center. Imagine seven sons and three daughters . . . lost! And yet he prays. He prays against God. He prays for his friends who had betrayed him for the sake of their orthodoxy. He prays . . . and suffers . . . and lives on.

Questions for Reflection and Discussion

1. How do we pray when we think God is unfair?
2. What questions does God ask us in prayer?
3. For whom else should we pray when God answers us?

Retrospect

From this set of prayers that I have exposited in some detail, some conclusions may be drawn. I intend that this retrospect—tilted toward theological substance—should be a match for my introductory comments that are more critically inclined. Thus I suggest that my thinking has moved from *the critical*—through textual exposition—toward *the theological:*

1. The God addressed in Israel's prayers is a full player in a thick and daring transaction. This means that the God addressed does not conform to the safe, settled categories of much Christian theology found in the doctrinal traditions and in the catechisms of the church. Whereas much of the church's delineation of the God of the gospel is given in the more static terms of Western philosophy, this God—not surprisingly—is cast in Jewish terms. This casting permits God to be variously elusive, irascible, open to impingement, and capable of disjunctive response. This God is celebrated and counted upon to be steadfast and compassionate; much prayer in Israel arises precisely from the lived reality that God does not always perform in such ways . . . thus the urgent crisis context of prayer.[1] As a result, much prayer in Israel is a prayer for presence in the face of divine absence, summoning God back to God's best, trusted qualities.[2]

2. Because of the character of this God, the engagement of

Israel in prayer is a genuine interactive dialogue. The capacity for such engagement is rooted in the covenant of Sinai to which YHWH is centrally committed. It is on the basis of that divine commitment and exchange of mutual covenantal vows that Israel dares to address and petition this God, a practice immediately undertaken by Moses in Exodus 32:11–14. This dialogic transaction that marks Israel's prayers is thick and complex; but most of all, it is *real* according to Israel's best faith. This transaction is not to be understood in terms of classic theological claims of God's "omniscience" and "omnipresence," for it is exactly that God *does not know* and God *is not present* that evokes much of Israel's prayer.[3] I suspect that in the Western church, beguiled as it is by a "perennial theology" that treats God as object rather than subject, this point is crucial concerning biblical prayer. The attempt to situate prayer in the context of conventional Western theology has caused prayer to be anemic and polite, and without urgent expectation, because there is a quality of unreality about prayer with a God who is "omni." From such a theological assumption, the impact of prayer is frequently taken to be upon the one who prays, because the God addressed is already, by definition, out beyond our prayers.

Ancient Israel did not accept such anemic and polite prayer, but believed that something real and urgent is at stake in prayer. In our own contemporary experience, moreover, that same sense that something urgent is at stake in prayer is evidenced in the urgency of prayer when one is pushed, by circumstance, to regressive speech. In such a moment, we may regress behind what is anemic and polite to utterance that may be rude and demanding and vigorous. While we in our contemporeneity may do so only in acute emergency, such prayer is recurring in ancient Israel. Prayer that centers in petition is an act that summons God and insists on God's attentive responsiveness. The rhetorical tradition of Israel indicates that, in more ways than we understand, Israel did receive divine response, at least enough to sustain the practice.

3. Because of *the full play of the character of God* in prayer and, consequently, because of *the serious interactive, dialogic quality of*

prayer, Israel, in its prayer, can engage in full candor and in honest pursuit of self-interest. There is no pretence or posturing in such prayer.

In its *practice of candor*, Israel is able to tell the truth about its life without camouflage or decoration. It is true that in ancient Israel YHWH is the God "from whom no secret can be hid"; but even more important, YHWH is the God from whom no secret need be hid. For that reason Israel's prayers tell God, in vivid and even hyperbolic rhetoric, exactly the problem and exactly what needs to be done. The most extravagant case of the latter is in Psalm 109:6–20, wherein the speaker details for God what must be done to the adversary.[4] Some of Israel's prayers border on paranoia, precisely because Israel holds back nothing in its extreme circumstance.

In its *pursuit of self-interest*, Israel is capable of expressing its need with great desperation and, on occasion, self-pity. But Israel's pursuit of self-interest is at times also quite knowing, so that such prayer can offer motivation to YHWH for YHWH's action, thus proposing to YHWH that YHWH's own interest is at stake along with the interest of the petitioner. Thus the prayers sometimes suggest that the interest of Israel and the interest of God may converge, because YHWH is understood in Israel as a God who is eager for praise and anxious about humiliation and shame before the other gods and the other nations. The appeal to divine self-interest obviously has no place in a theology of the God who is "omni." But this God, in Israel's purview, knows about self-promotion and self-advancement, and so can be engaged at the point of Israel's need.

4. Israel's prayers can be intimate and quite personal, geared to the need and circumstance of the one who prays. But such personal prayers are never in a vacuum. Any Israelite who prays does so as a member of the community of Israel and so appeals to the memory and the common rhetorical practice of Israel. Thus the prayer of every Israelite is a prayer of all Israel, for no individual person can step outside of membership in that community. This permits the individual prayer to appeal to the larger tradition, and

also to summon "the congregation" to be present to the immediacy of the prayer. The interface of individual and community poses no problem in ancient Israel, and is only a problem in the context of modern "autonomy." Thus the recovery of a communal (ecclesial) sense of urgent, demanding, and sometimes rude prayer is important in contemporary communities of prayer where prayer has become excessively anemic and polite.

5. The capacity of the individual Israelite to pray as a member of the community permits prayer to take a very long view of life with YHWH. Thus prayer is often poignantly related to a specific circumstance, but such particular circumstance is situated, in the imaginative act of prayer, in the long story of Israel's life with YHWH. The individual person does not pray in isolation or in a vacuum, but as a part of the *long memory* of miracle and the *long hope* of promised well-being. The present circumstance of the one who prays is radically redefined by the extent of memory and the extent of hope, both of which are palpably available in every circumstance of the well-grounded Israelite.

6. Even given the communal dimension of prayer and the setting of prayer in Israel's long-term memory and hope, Israel's prayers are highly contextual. Because the prayers of petition arise in circumstances of threat, need, shame, abandonment, and exposure, the prayers concern that moment of crisis. The crisis is described and a divine antidote is sought when the petitioner has run out of options of his or her own. Thus the prayers are remarkable acts of imagination that make connections between *the thick faith of Israel* and *the immediacy of critical context*. It is that connection that has a chance to mobilize the God of Israel for the moment of need, in the conviction that when God enters any circumstance, everything will be changed by active *intervention*, but changed, as well, simply by *presence*.

7. At the center of prayer is the imperative on the lips of Israel. This practice of imperative petition is so familiar to us that we may take it for granted and not notice the daring quality of such utterance. Such utterance is an act of a needy Israelite, often bereft of resources or credentials, with the freedom and the

courage to ask. It as though in this moment the petitioner dares to take the upper hand in relation to YHWH and "commands" YHWH to act. Of course we do not like to think of petition in this way. But in regressive moments of emergency, we do cast off much inhibition and "cut to the chase." In an emergency, a human agent with courage may assume a "commanding" position. In an appeal to Matthew 7:7, Karl Barth reminds us that prayer is all about "asking."[5] If we do not ask, we do not receive. The wonder of the interaction is that YHWH, at the other end of the dialogue, is willing to engage in such an exchange and is willing to be the one addressed and "commanded" by Israel's imperative. Of course it is the case that YHWH continues to exercise freedom in the relationship and is not an automaton, even as Israel maintains its freedom in the relationship. Even given that divine freedom, however, Israel knows and trusts that YHWH's fidelity causes a tilt of YHWH's freedom toward transformative engagement. Confidence in that divine tilt is the ground of Israel's daring petition.

Such prayer strikes us as odd because it is so "primitive." It is odd in the midst of Enlightenment rationality; it is odd in the Western church, which has inhaled deeply of modern rationality. In the context of Israel's prayer, we may recognize that modern Enlightenment rationality is a practice through which the human spirit shrivels and the prospect for human community is diminished. A recovery of a dialogic, transactive practice of prayer is urgent for faithful practice in the church. It is equally urgent for the recovery of humanness in a society too much inured to technical management that eschews the most elemental, sacramental dimensions of humanness.

I conclude with one other observation. The "primitive" practice of prayer—largely nullified through modernist rationality—has been kept alive through the psychoanalytic legacy of Sigmund Freud. While it is clear that Freud's legacy has passed through a variety of decisive modifications—notably with object relations theory—one cannot get away from the defining influence of Freud, who understood so well the hidden, thick interaction that makes for humanness.[6] On the one hand, Freud is deeply rooted in a Jewish practice of *layered interpretation*, a practice congruent with rabbinic approaches to texts. On the other hand, Freud understood the Jewish tradition of *dialogic interaction* through verbal exchange, an interaction that stands in profound contrast to the Greek tradition of rational thought. It is the legacy of *thick interpretation* and *verbal dialogic interaction* that are at the heart of Freud's insight. Both of these aspects of his legacy are important; either without the other will not work.

It is crucial to see that the twinned enterprise of *thick interpretation* and verbal *dialogic interaction* are, in ancient Israel, rooted in covenant that is practiced in prayer in which YHWH is the formidable and indispensable dialogic partner. It is with YHWH that Israel interpreted its life and engaged in rhetorical exercises toward transformation. While Freud traveled in rich ways in this tradition, he clearly needed, in late modern European culture, to appreciate this most human of all transactions apart from YHWH as either agent or partner. The outcome is "talk therapy" in which the therapist assumes the role of YHWH as the one with faithful authority who hears and responds. In recent time, moreover, those who reflect on this practice have discerned that the therapist, the defining dialogic partner, is not, need not be, and cannot be "omni," but is party to the risk of the exercise.

I wish in no way to denigrate such therapeutic transactions, for I am a major beneficiary of such a process. But in the context of the present discussion, the reference to the legacy of Freud leads us to remember that the practice of prayer in synagogue and in church is an older, thicker, and more "primitive" practice from the rootage of Israel's covenantalism. In contemporary practice I do not believe that prayer and "talk therapy" constitute an either/or. But the more elite practice of talk therapy is rooted in and shaped by the more elemental, more democratic practice of prayer. To understand prayer through the legacy of Freud in his Jewishness is to appropriate the "primitive" dimension of prayer. It also entails a decisive recharacterization of prayer and a break with the anemic inclination of much contemporary prayer. Freud understood, as did ancient Israel long before him, that this dialogic transaction is a life-or-death matter, most especially so in a culture that seeks to stop all human "primitive" engagement. That it is a life-or-death matter is why the blind beggar (Mark 10:46–52) and the widow (Luke 18:1–8) refused to desist from their engagement with transformative power. Such "primitive" practice is the way in which the faithful have always refused to "lose heart" (Luke 18:1).

Notes

Introduction

1. J. Wentzel van Huyssteen, *Alone in the World? Human Uniqueness in Science and Theology* (Gifford Lectures; Grand Rapids: Eerdmans, 2006), 165–215.
2. Ibid., 251, 259.
3. Witness the exuberant public response to regime collapse under Marcos in the Philippines and under Ceauşescu in Rumania.
4. Lindsey Crittenden, *The Water Will Hold You: A Skeptic Learns to Pray* (New York: Harmony Books, 2007), 18.
5. On the intimate interface of body and voice, see Elaine Scarry, *The Body in Pain: The Making and Unmaking of the World* (Oxford: Oxford University Press, 1985), chap. 4. Scarry's analysis is poignant for our theme. She is, in my judgment, in error in this verdict on p. 219: "The body in the Old Testament belongs only to man, and the voice, in its extreme and unqualified form, belongs only to God." At the outset of the narrative of the exodus, the commanding voice is that of Israel, which evokes a divine voice of promise in response.
6. There may be good reason not to name the name on critical grounds. In the telling of the Exodus narrative, the name is not clarified until Exod. 3:13–15 and Exod. 6:2–3. That apparent decision in the shaping of the tradition, however, does not detract from the character of the prayer of the slaves, a voice of pain addressed to no God in particular.
7. James L. Kugel, *The God of Old: Inside the Lost World of the Bible* (New York: Free Press, 2003), 124.
8. Ibid., 129–30.
9. Ibid., 135–36.

10. Notice the jarring statement of realism by Kugel (pp. 128–29) through which he acknowledges, "Sometimes He listens, sometimes He doesn't." Kugel's judgment is surely correct: remarkably, such data did "not flash Disconnect" for Israel.

11. Friedrich Heiler, *Prayer: A Study in the History and Psychology of Religion* (London: Oxford University Press, 1932).

12. See Michael J. Buckley, *At the Origins of Modern Atheism* (New Haven, CT: Yale University Press, 1987), who traces the philosophical argument through which atheism became a live option in the West, an option that resisted all that was "primitive" in faith.

13. Heiler, *Prayer*, 95.

14. Ibid., 96.

15. Ibid., 98.

16. Ibid., 99.

17. Ibid.

18. Ibid., 103. See the discussion of David Crump, *Knocking on Heaven's Door: A New Testament Theology of Petitionary Prayer* (Grand Rapids: Baker Academic Press, 2006), and the way in which he moves from the generic categories of Heiler to the specificity of the New Testament.

19. Alongside praise, Israel's prayers often culminate in thanksgiving. The relationship between praise and thanksgiving in Israel's rhetoric is a close and delicate one, but in actual usage the two are often conflated and taken together.

20. The "magnification" of YHWH through praise indicates the dramatic assumptions of such prayer (see Pss. 34:3; 69:30). The assumption is that Israel's praise, like cheerleading, enhances YHWH in competition with other gods or before other peoples. Thus, for example, in Ps. 22:6, YHWH is "enthroned" on the praises of Israel, that is, elevated by their singing so that YHWH's throne is raised above the thrones of YHWH's competitors.

21. Thus Harold Fisch, *Poetry with a Purpose: Biblical Poetics and Interpretation* (Bloomington: Indiana University Press, 1990) 108–9.

22. Hermann Gunkel, *An Introduction to the Psalms* (Macon, GA: Mercer University Press, 1998). The most important study of Israel's prayers is by Patrick D. Miller, *They Cried to the Lord: The Form and Theology of Biblical Prayer* (Minneapolis: Fortress Press, 1994). Miller has organized his study around the genres identified by Gunkel.

23. See Walter Brueggemann, "The Formfulness of Grief," in idem, *The Psalms and the Life of Faith*, ed. Patrick D. Miller (Minneapolis: Fortress Press, 1995), 84–97.

24. See George W. Stroup, *Before God* (Grand Rapids: Eerdmans, 2004).

25. The silence of which I write is the imposed silence of repression and oppression. Clearly the laden silence that operates in serious contemplative prayer is completely of another kind.

26. My citations concern current critical discussion of these prayers. For a very different approach to Jewish prayer in Hasidic tradition, see *Your Word Is Fire: The Hasidic Masters on Contemplative Prayer*, ed. and trans. Arthur Green and Barry W. Holtz (New York: Schocken Books, 1987). I am grateful to Hugh Ward for this reference.
27. Moshe Greenberg, *Biblical Prose Prayer as a Window to the Popular Religion of Ancient Israel* (Berkeley: University of California Press, 1983).
28. Ibid., 20.
29. Ibid., 11.
30. Ronald E. Clements, *In Spirit and in Truth: Insights from Biblical Prayers* (Atlanta: John Knox Press, 1985).
31. Ibid., 5–6.
32. Ibid., 6.
33. In *They Cried to the Lord*, Miller's chapter headings, for those who know about the genres, refer directly to the familiar genres of the prayers of the Psalter.
34. Miller, *They Cried to the Lord*, 304–35.
35. Samuel E. Balentine, *Prayer in the Hebrew Bible: The Drama of Divine-Human Dialogue* (Overtures to Biblical Theology; Minneapolis: Fortress Press, 1993).
36. Ibid., 288.
37. Karl Barth, *Prayer*, with essays by John Hesselink, et al.; trans. Sara F. Terrien (Philadelphia: Westminster Press, 1952), 13.
38. Karl Barth, *Church Dogmatics* III 3 (Edinburgh: T & T Clark, 1961), 268.
39. Clements, *In Spirit and in Truth*, 10.
40. Karl Barth, *Prayer: With Essays by I. John Hesselink, Daniel L. Migliore, and Donald K. McKim* (50th Anniversary Ed.; Louisville: Westminster John Knox Press, 2002), 13.
41. The clearest case in which Israel remembers old divine fidelities as the basis for future divine fidelities is Lam. 3:21–24.
42. George Steiner, *Real Presences* (Chicago: University of Chicago Press, 1989), 225, comments: "It is the Hebraic intuition that God is capable of all speech-acts except that of monologue, which has generated our arts of reply, of questioning and counter-creation."

Retrospect

1. The book of Job is the obvious case in which God does not perform according to expectation. The argument of the book turns on the contention of the friends that Job has defaulted; as the argument goes along, Job eventually breaks ranks with his friends and doubts God's reliability to do what God has promised (see Job 9:19–24).
2. This is the general thesis of Fredrik Lindström, *Suffering and Sin: Interpretations of Illness in the Individual Complaint Psalms* (Coniectanea biblica:

Old Testament Series 37; Stockholm: Almqvist & Wiksell International, 1994).

3. The textual data has been carefully reviewed by Terence E. Fretheim, *The Suffering of God: An Old Testament Perspective* (Overtures to Biblical Theology; Philadelphia: Fortress Press, 1984).

4. There is an interesting textual or interpretive problem connected with these verses in Ps. 109. Many interpreters prefer to place these vitriolic words in the mouth of the opponent; they do so by inserting "they say" in v. 6, an inclination followed by the NRSV. The matter is finessed by Norbert Lohfink, *In the Shadow of Your Wings: New Readings of Great Texts from the Bible* (Collegeville, MN: Liturgical Press, 2003), 120, by inserting a colon after v. 5 and placing vv. 6–19 in quotes. While not as blatant, this procedure also amounts to a particular interpretive slant for which there is no clear warrant in the text.

5. Karl Barth, *Church Dogmatics* III 3 (Edinburgh: T & T Clark, 1961), 268:

    In the first instance, it is an asking, a seeking and knocking directed towards God; a wishing, a desiring and a requesting presented to God. . . . But it is the fact that he comes before God with his petition, which makes him a praying man. Other theories of prayer may be richly and profoundly thought out and may sound very well, but they all suffer from a certain artificiality because they miss this simple and concrete fact, losing themselves in heights and depths where there is no place for the man who really prays, who is simply making a request.

6. The transformation of Freud's understanding into an interpersonal interactive model has been accomplished through object relations theory, on which see D. W. Winnicott, *The Maturational Processes and the Facilitating Environment: Studies in the Theory of Emotional Development* (Madison, CT: International Universities Press, 1965).